Chinese FOOD
& FOLKLORE

Jeni Wright

NOTES
Standard level spoon measurements are used in all recipes.
1 tablespoon = one 15 ml spoon
1 teaspoon = one 5 ml spoon

Eggs should be medium unless otherwise stated.

Ovens should be preheated to the specified temperature—if using a convection oven, follow the manufacturer's instructions for adjusting the time and temperature.

Acknowledgments
The author would like to thank Yvonne Deutsch for her invaluable assistance. She would also like to thank her family and friends for their help with tasting all the recipes as they were tested.

Jacket Recipe
Tangarine Beef. See page 78.

Publishing Director Laura Bamford
Editor Katey Day
Copy Editor Anne Crane
Art Director Keith Martin
Senior Designer Leigh Jones
Production Controller Katherine Hockley

Contributors
Photographer Ian Wallace
Home Economist Sunil Vijayakar
Stylist Wei Tang
Picture Researcher Wendy Gay
Indexer Hilary Bird

North American Edition
Publisher Allen Orso
Managing Editor JoAnn Padgett
Project Editor Elizabeth McNulty

Published in the United States by
Laurel Glen Publishing
5880 Oberlin Drive, Suite 400
San Diego, CA 92121-4794

First published in 1999 by Hamlyn
an imprint of Octopus Publishing Group Limited
2-4 Heron Quays, London E14 4JP

ISBN 1-57145-640-6

Library of Congress Cataloging-in-Publication Data available upon request.

Printed in China by Toppan Printing Co., (H.K.) Ltd.

Contents

introduction

"To ordinary people, food is tantamount to heaven." This was a shrewd observation made by a Chinese government official in 200 BC. At that time, close to the end of the great Chou dynasty, the special place of food in Chinese life was clearly

appreciation of food has been raised to the level of a high philosophy.

CHINESE CIVILIZATION

Chinese civilization stretches right back to the realms of folklore. It is described in mythology as beginning with

people how to fish, hunt, grow crops, and cook. Although the Xia civilization was mentioned in early Chinese historical texts, the best archaeological evidence of an early dynasty is of the Shang dynasty, which followed, and ruled in, areas of northern and central China. Its capital city was Anyang near the border of Hunan. The Shang dynasty was renowned for its skills in agriculture, as well as the development of a system of writing, which has been found in inscriptions on tortoise shells and cattle bones. They also made great advances in metallurgy: bronze ships, weapons, and tools from the era have been found at Bronze Age sites at Anyang.

acknowledged. Intriguingly, Chou dynasty texts mention the use of the *ting* cauldron, a common cooking vessel, as the symbol of the state. Food has always been important in China's history, especially during the terrible periods of famine and hardship. However, its meaning in Chinese culture is far more fascinating than issues of basic sustenance. Here, the preparation and

Pangu, the creator of the universe. Pangu was followed by a series of legendary, wise emperors and heroes—fabled beings who were said to have brought the gifts of communication and vital survival techniques to the ancient Chinese. During the Xia dynasty, which existed 2000 years before the birth of Christ, the legendary Emperor Fu was said to have taught his

From these distant origins to the present day, China's astonishingly long history has been full of color and incident. A succession of imperious lords, overlords, Kings and Emperors, with their sumptuous courts and gorgeous palaces enacted their various dramas over 4000 years of 16 major dynasties (which were themselves subdivided into distinct periods). The final dynasty (the Ch'ing) ended with the death of the last Emperor in 1911. Much of world history inevitably centers around wars and conquests, invasions and heroic feats, and China has its own quota of these. However, one of the most enduring threads throughout the thousands of years of Chinese history has been the great emphasis placed on key systems of thought and philosophy, and the important status given to the thinker in day-to-day life. It may come as a considerable surprise to those who appreciate Chinese cuisine that no less a person than the great sage Confucius had very pronounced ideas about the meaning of food in life.

The Golden Age

Confucius (551–479 BC) was a key figure of the great classical age of China, the Chou dynasty (1122–221 BC). This dynasty ruled during a period of tumultuous conflict and civil disorder, yet at the same time it witnessed an era of amazing cultural prosperity: the "golden age" of China. A tidal wave of reform and new concepts went side by side with major economic and technological advances. The ruler delegated the running of the empire to regional, and often fiercely competing, warlords who themselves were in dire need of educated, literate officials to put these ideas into action. There was growing prosperity too: commercial transactions were now much easier because of the invention of coinage, and iron had begun to be used for the manufacture of such diverse items as weapons, tools, and farm implements. Enormous public works were undertaken, including flood control schemes, irrigation

projects, and canal building. It was at this time that huge walls were built around cities and along large tracts of the northern frontier.

The Hundred Schools of Thought

The newly emerging officials-cum-intellectuals sought by these regional rulers played a crucial role in this period. It is not surprising, therefore, that a kaleidoscope of philosophies developed, and that the era is often known as the "Hundred Schools of Thought." Most of the core texts on which Chinese ethical and moral codes were based for the following 2500 years emerged from this time. Many of these philosophers traveled about the kingdom: they acted as sages and consultants to various regional lords on the rules of conduct, government, war, and diplomacy, while at the same time they taught moral philosophy and ethics.

The Confucian School

The Confucian School of thought was destined to be the theoretical foundation of a code outlining the orderly structure of traditional Chinese society. Confucius postulated that an ideal social and political order would result if each person were to act according to formally prescribed relationships. "Let the ruler be a ruler and the subject a subject," he famously wrote. However, he pointed out that for this principle to work, the King as head of society must behave impeccably. In his eyes, the stratification of society was a reality that had to be informed by ethical values. He advanced the case for the "gentleman," the cultivated or superior man. In his view, the cultivated man would be as concerned with the order, beauty, and harmony of the food on his table as he would with the details of a diplomatic feud.

In fact, Confucius held the art of cooking in high esteem. Within his writings he discussed the fine details of culinary procedures and table etiquette. Even in the present era, many of these customs are very familiar. The tradition of cutting food into small, bite-sized pieces while it is being prepared rather than when it is on the plate is unique to Chinese cuisine. Chopsticks rather than knives are considered to be the perfect eating implement. In accordance with his teachings

on harmony and structure, Confucius taught that good cooking depends on the careful balance of various ingredients and flavorings—no single flavor from the ingredients should stand out. Without this harmony there is no taste, in both senses of the word. He also said that color and texture were vital in the presentation of food.

Food at the Court

The importance of food in court culture was already long established before Confucius lived. Around 1115 BC an expert in nutrition was a key member of the imperial court; he was also responsible for health matters. This official not only supervised the Emperor's chefs, but also investigated the influences of different foods and ingredients on the emotional and physical health of the court. Based on comparatively few ingredients, a staggering variety of recipes were created. This intense

curiosity about food, its various effects and refined pleasures, laid the foundations of a recognizable gourmet tradition. Confucius was directly in line with this tradition when he said that the enjoyment of food is one of the ways to bring about peace and harmony in society. This was why the court official who linked food and heaven was so sure of his ground. He knew how important food was and that the ordinary people would be contented when they had plenty.

Taoism

The other great influential philosophy in Chinese culture was the Tao (pronounced 'Dao'). Taoism was the second most important thread of Chinese thought, and it also emerged during the Chou period. Its origin is attributed to the venerable sage Lao Zi (Old Master), who probably lived before Confucius. Zhuang Zi (369–286 BC) further developed the theory. Taoism concentrates on the place of the individual in the natural order of the universe rather than in the social order. It teaches that the aim in life for the individual is to identify one's own unique place in the rhythm of the natural and spiritual worlds and by this means to follow the Way (Tao) of the universe. Interestingly, for some people, Taoism acted as a counterbalance to Confucian conformity. For example, a scholar posted in an official capacity would tend to follow Confucian principles in his official conduct. In his private life, however, he might follow the Way, then, after retirement, he might decide to become a Taoist recluse. Like Confucianism, Taoism connected with many important principles that had gone before. For example, two of the principal preoccupations of this philosophy were the effect of nutrition on the body and the quest for longevity. This harks back to the fascination with nutritional matters at the imperial court. Taoists were immensely concerned with the life-giving attributes of various foods. They also held strong views on the health aspects of food preparation.

FOOD AS MEDICINE

It is clear that the connection between food and medicine is central to the major strands of Chinese thinking. The other major theory underpinning

this is the concept of yin-yang. This philosophy also emerged during the Chou dynasty and evolved into a theory of the five elements. Believers defined the universe in terms of basic forces in nature. These were complementary forces of

yin (dark, cold, female, negative) and yang (light, hot, male, positive) expressed through the five elements (water, fire, wood, metal, and earth). Later these theories became mainstream beliefs. In this theory, the body is influenced by basic yin-yang principles. Many foods can also be classified as having yin or yang qualities. If the yin and yang forces in the body are out of equilibrium, the body becomes unhealthy. To resolve this, the correct amounts and kinds of foods must be taken to counterbalance the yin and

yang upset. In a healthy person, overeating any one food would result in an excess of its influence in the body, and this would cause disease.

The Chinese people hardly make any distinction between food and medicine. This explains the staggering variety of ingredients used in traditional Chinese medicine, reflected in the Imperial Cookbook of the Mongol dynasty, in which there are chapters devoted to preserving long life and warding off disease. In one example, a man is not supposed to have lustful desires while eating a lotus seed: this would neutralize the purifying powers of the seed. The theory of the "'harmonization of foods" can be traced back to the Shang dynasty, which predated the Chou dynasty. The sage Yi Yin connected the five flavors

of sweet, sour, bitter, spicy hot, and salty to the nutritional needs of the body's five major organ systems (the heart, liver, spleen/pancreas, lungs, and kidneys), and stressed their role in maintaining good physical health.

MEDICINAL FOODS

Many of the plants used in Chinese cooking—spring onions (scallions), root ginger, garlic, dried lily buds, tree fungus, for example—all have known value in preventing and alleviating illnesses. Over the centuries the Chinese have explored the world of plants, roots, herbs, fungi, and seeds. They have found that the nutritional value of vegetables can be destroyed by over-

cooking and that many food items have curative properties. Ginger, a favorite spice, is now commonly used to calm an upset stomach and to combat colds. This is all based on the deep knowledge the Chinese have acquired about their native plants. This knowledge is not restricted to intellectuals—the majority of Chinese peasants know every edible plant in their neighborhood. This knowledge has been handed down through the centuries as a living culture, and is still alive today.

FAN AND TS'AI

In Chinese food culture, there is one golden rule in the preparation of food. It is vital that there is a correct balance

of ingredients in every meal based on *fan* ingredients— grains and other starchy foods, and *ts'ai* ingredients— vegetables and meat. The Chinese cook aims to have the correct proportions of *fan* and *ts'ai*, so the ingredients are prepared ahead with this in mind. For the *fan* element in a dish, grains may be served cooked whole or as flour, steamed rice may be served, cornbread is suitable, as are pancakes and noodles. Vegetables and meats are chopped up and combined into individual dishes to represent the *ts'ai* part of the meal. In the kitchen there are *fan* utensils and *ts'ai* utensils, both for cooking and for serving. The chopping knife or cleaver and the chopping block are standard equipment in every Chinese kitchen.

REGIONAL DISHES

Many Chinese dishes, for example Ants Climbing Trees, Ma-Po Tofu, and Steamed Whole Fish, have entertaining stories connected to them, which have endless associations in popular culture. In the case of the more common dishes, the stories are deftly changed to fit local characters and locations. By contrast, there are the sacred regional classics. For example, although there are many kinds of Chinese roast duck recipes, Peking (or Beijing) Duck is unique.

As China is so huge and has such a rich and complex history, a huge variety of culinary styles has evolved. The main styles are relatively familiar to the West; they include Beijing, Cantonese, Sichuan, and Huaiyang. Every region claims that theirs is the best cuisine, but because Chinese people are so curious and passionate about food, most of them will try dishes from different areas. In the case of Cantonese food, they may tread warily, however. The Cantonese are renowned for eating almost anything. In the local markets you will find all manner of creatures destined for the kitchen, including dogs, snakes, cats, and owls. A famous Cantonese saying boasts that anything with four legs and its back facing the sky can be eaten—apart from the table.

Beijing

For centuries the imperial court was centered in Beijing, and the Emperors had the finest cooks at their service; accordingly, Beijing cuisine is inevitably influenced by the imperial cooking schools. The region was invaded by Tartar and Mongol peoples, who brought with them their Muslim traditions and their flocks of sheep. Consequently, mutton and lamb dishes are unique to this area.

Canton

When the Ming dynasty was overthrown in 1644, the court fled south to Canton, and the court chefs gradually merged their Beijing style with that of Canton. The result is one of the most varied and exciting cuisines in China.

Sichuan

Sichuan food is so spicy, it may make your eyes water. It is food that is admirably suited to the climate—it helps you to perspire in the hot, humid summers and keeps you warm in the bitterly cold winters. Sichuan cookery is also renowned for its pungent salty preserves. Other hot and spicy cooking styles are found in Hunan and Jiangxi cuisines, both famous for their liberal use of chilies.

Huaiyang

The area on the eastern coast of China bordering the East China Sea has some of the most fertile land in the country. The cuisine makes extensive use of its fresh fruit and vegetables and abundant seafood. The other major regions of eastern China are Nanking, which is renowned for its succulent duck recipes, and Shanghai, which has a cuisine that delights in mellow, slightly sweet flavors. Sweet and sour dishes are typical of Shanghai cookery.

Whatever region you explore in China, you are likely to be greeted with the phrase "Chi fan le mei yo?" which literally means "Have you eaten yet?" What Chinese people are really wanting to know is that all is well with you. In this wise, ancient culture, where food was said to be tantamount to heaven all those thousands of years ago, no other greeting could be so full of profound meaning.

soups, starters, & snacks

The sociable Chinese adore visiting their local teahouse to sample the delicious savory bites and snacks available there. These usually include wontons, various kinds of dumplings, and spring rolls. Along with the food, they exchange titbits of gossip and consume vast quantities of hot tea. Soups of all kinds are popular in China, especially when made with fragrant fresh stocks and scented with the fabulous spicy flavors of chili, ginger, and coriander.

Hot & Sour Soup

about ½ oz. dried shiitake
    mushrooms
½ cup hot water
¼–⅓ lb. boneless cooked chicken
3½ cups Chicken Stock (see p. 14)
2 tablespoons rice wine vinegar or
    white wine or cider vinegar, or
    more to taste
2 tablespoons light soy sauce, or
    more to taste
1 teaspoon sugar
1 red chili, deseeded and very
    finely sliced or chopped
4 scallions, very finely sliced on the
    diagonal
2 teaspoons cornstarch

Very popular in the West, especially in restaurants, this warming soup can traditionally be quite complicated with lots of different ingredients, but this is a quick-and-easy version, made hot with fresh red chili rather than the more usual pepper.

1 Soak the dried mushrooms in the hot water for 35–40 minutes. Drain the mushrooms in a sieve over a bowl and reserve the soaking water. Finely slice the mushrooms, discarding any hard stalks. With your fingers, shred the cooked chicken.

2 Bring the stock to a boil in a large saucepan. Add 2 tablespoons each of vinegar and soy sauce, then add the sugar, mushrooms, and strained soaking water. Simmer for 5 minutes. Add half the chili and scallions, stir well and simmer for 5 minutes more.

3 Add the shredded chicken, stir and heat through for 1–2 minutes. Blend the cornstarch to a paste with a little cold water, then pour it into the soup and stir to mix. Simmer, stirring, for 1–2 minutes until the soup thickens.

4 Taste and add more vinegar and/or soy sauce, to make the soup as sour and salty as you like. Serve piping hot, sprinkled with the remaining chili and scallions.

Cook's Notes
This is a good soup to make if you have some leftover roast chicken, or to use the poached chicken meat from making Chicken Stock (page 14).

Serves 6–8
Preparation time: 10 minutes, plus soaking
Cooking time: about 15 minutes

'Every book must be chewed to get out its juice.'

Chinese Proverb

Chicken Stock

1 small chicken, weighing about
   2 lb.
½ lemon, cut into chunks
1 inch fresh ginger
4 scallions
salt

Good stock is essential for Chinese soups because they are invariably simple, relying on the stock to provide a flavorsome backdrop for thinly sliced or chopped fresh ingredients. This stock is fresh and lemony, and it goes well with the soups in this chapter, but you can play around with the flavoring ingredients, adding more or less lemon, ginger, and scallions, or even omitting them, as you like.

1 Wash the chicken under cold running water. Place the lemon chunks in the body cavity of the chicken. Put the chicken breast-side down in a large saucepan and cover generously with cold water (you will need about 3 quarts). Bring the water to a boil over a moderate heat.

2 Meanwhile, slice the ginger, but do not peel it, and cut the scallions crossways into thirds or quarters.

3 Skim off any scum from the surface of the water. Add the ginger, scallions, and a pinch of salt, then half-cover the pan. Turn the heat down to low and simmer the stock gently for for 2–3 hours. Turn the chicken over from time to time and skim any scum off the surface of the stock.

4 Remove the chicken from the stock, then boil the stock rapidly for about 30 minutes to reduce and concentrate it slightly. Strain the stock through a muslin-lined sieve and leave to cool. Refrigerate overnight, then lift any fat off the surface. Use as required.

Cook's Notes
Some cooks add raw pork rib bones to the chicken, or use all pork and no chicken, depending on the intended use of the stock.

Don't waste the chicken meat. Strip it off the bones and use it for soups and salads. It is perfect for Hot & Sour Soup (page 12) and Bonbonji (page 64).

Makes about 3 cups
Preparation time: 10 minutes, plus cooling and chilling
Cooking time: 2½–3½ hours

Egg Flower Soup

This delicate, pretty-sounding soup sometimes goes by the name of Egg Drop Soup. It is very simple and quick.

1 Put the stock, scallions, soy sauce, and sugar into a large saucepan and bring to a boil.

2 Beat the eggs in a small bowl with the oil and a little salt and pepper. Pour the eggs into the boiling soup and break them up into threads by stirring with chopsticks or a fork. Remove the pan from the heat, cover with the lid, and let stand for about 1 minute before serving.

Cook's Notes

If you don't have homemade chicken stock, you can cheat by using canned concentrated chicken or beef consommé diluted with an equal volume of water.

Serves 4–6
Preparation time: 5 minutes
Cooking time: 7–8 minutes

3½ cups Chicken Stock (see p. 14)
2 scallions, very thinly sliced on the diagonal
2 teaspoons light soy sauce
½ teaspoon sugar
2 eggs
1 teaspoon sesame oil
salt and pepper

Crab Soup

3½ cups Chicken Stock (see p. 14)
1 inch piece of fresh ginger, peeled and very finely chopped
2 ripe tomatoes, skinned, deseeded, and very finely chopped
½ small red or green chili, deseeded and very finely chopped
2 tablespoons rice wine or dry sherry
1 tablespoon rice wine vinegar or white wine or cider vinegar
½ teaspoon sugar
1 tablespoon cornstarch
about 5 oz. white crabmeat, defrosted and drained thoroughly if frozen
salt and pepper
2 scallions, finely sliced, to garnish

Sweet and sour flavors go well with crab, so too does peppery hot ginger. Here, in this delicate soup, the combination makes an exquisite and harmonious balance.

1 Put the stock into a large saucepan with the ginger, tomatoes, chili, rice wine or sherry, vinegar and sugar. Bring to a boil; cover the pan and simmer for about 10 minutes to allow the flavors to mingle and mellow.
2 Blend the cornstarch to a paste with a little cold water, then pour it into the soup and stir to mix. Simmer, stirring, for 1–2 minutes until the soup thickens.
3 Add the crabmeat, stir gently to mix, then heat through for 2–3 minutes. Taste and add salt and pepper if necessary. Serve piping hot, sprinkled with the sliced scallions.

Cook's Notes
Most supermarkets sell whole cooked fresh crab seasonally and frozen white crabmeat year round. If you live near the ocean, you may be able to buy a whole cooked fresh crab from a local fishmonger and get him to remove the meat for you.

Serves 4–6
Preparation time: 10 minutes
Cooking time: about 20 minutes

Sweet & Spicy Spareribs

1 garlic clove
1 star anise
1 inch piece of fresh ginger, peeled
   and roughly chopped
2 tablespoons honey
2 tablespoons sugar
2 tablespoons chili sauce
2 tablespoons soy sauce
about 2 lb. pork spareribs
½ cup orange juice

You can buy ready-made spareribs in supermarkets, but they are almost always disappointing. It's much better to make your own, and you'll find this recipe very easy. The flavor of star anise is quite distinct.

1 Crush the garlic, star anise, and ginger using a mortar and pestle, then mix in the honey, sugar, chili, sauce and soy sauce.
2 Put the spareribs into a roasting tin or baking dish and brush them with the sweet and spicy mixture until they are evenly coated.
3 Roast the spareribs in a preheated oven at 375°F for 30 minutes.
4 Pour about half of the orange juice over the ribs and stir to mix it with the cooking juices. Turn the ribs over so that the browned sides face downwards. Return to the oven for a further 20 minutes.
5 Repeat with the remaining orange juice, mixed with a little water if the ribs are very sticky and brown at this stage. Lower the oven temperature to 300°F and roast for a further 10 minutes or until the ribs are well browned.

Cook's Notes
Make sure to buy the Chinese-style spareribs rather than sparerib chops. They are widely available at supermarkets and butchers. You can prepare the ribs up to the end of step 2 and leave them to marinate in the refrigerator overnight.

Serves 4
Preparation time: 10 minutes
Cooking time: about 1 hour

Chicken & Sweetcorn Soup

Like chop suey and chow mein, this is not an original Chinese recipe. It was invented by Chinese immigrants in the United States. It is rich and filling, with slightly sweet undertones, and is best served on its own rather than as part of a Chinese meal. It makes a very good lunch or supper.

1 Cut the chicken into very small, thin strips, working across the grain. Whisk the egg white lightly in a bowl with a fork. Add the rice wine or sherry and the strips of chicken, then stir to mix.
2 Put the stock, creamed corn, and soy sauce into a large saucepan and bring to a boil. Add the chicken strips and stir to mix, then cover the pan and simmer for 5–7 minutes or until the chicken is tender and cooked through.
3 Blend the cornstarch to a paste with a little cold water, then pour it into the soup and stir to mix. Simmer, stirring, for 1–2 minutes until the soup thickens.
4 Taste for seasoning and add more soy sauce if you like. Serve piping hot, sprinkled liberally with pepper.

Cook's Notes
The thick, rich texture of creamed corn gives this soup body. If you prefer, you can also use ordinary canned corn instead and increase the amount of cornstarch by 1 teaspoon.

Serves 4–6
Preparation time: about 10 minutes
Cooking time: 10–15 minutes

1 large boneless, skinless chicken breast, weighing just under ½ lb.
1 egg white
2 tablespoons rice wine or dry sherry
4 cups Chicken Stock (see p. 14)
14 oz. cannned creamed corn
1 tablespoon light soy sauce, or more to taste
2 teaspoons cornstarch
salt and pepper

'A truly great man never puts away the simplicity of a child.'

Chinese Proverb

Raindrop Soup

3½ cups Chicken Stock (see p. 14)
2 tablespoons rice wine or dry
    sherry
7 oz. canned water chestnuts,
    drained and very thinly sliced
    into rounds
4 scallions (white part only), very
    thinly sliced into rings
¼ lb. cooked peeled shrimp,
    defrosted and dried thoroughly
    if frozen
salt and pepper
a few drops of sesame oil, to finish

1 Put the stock into a large saucepan and bring to a boil over a high heat. Stir in the rice wine or sherry, then add the water chestnuts and scallions and simmer for 2 minutes.
2 Turn the heat down to low and add the shrimp. Heat through gently for 1–2 minutes, then taste and season with salt and pepper if necessary. Serve piping hot, with little drops of sesame oil floating on top.

Serves 4–6
Preparation time: 5 minutes
Cooking time: 10 minutes

Sesame Shrimp Toasts

½ lb. cooked peeled shrimp,
    defrosted and dried thoroughly,
    if frozen
2 scallions, roughly chopped
2 garlic cloves, roughly chopped
2 tablespoons cornstarch
2 teaspoons soy sauce
12 slices of stale white bread (from
    a large, thick sliced loaf), crusts
    removed
6-8 tablespoons sesame seeds
about 2 cups peanut oil, for deep-
    frying
soy sauce, for dipping

Crisp and crunchy, these toasts make an interesting starter for a Chinese meal. If you are worried about deep-frying when guests arrive, you can make the shrimp toasts up to an hour before then crisp them up in a hot oven just before serving.

1 Grind the shrimp into a paste in a food processor with the scallions, garlic, cornstarch, and soy sauce.
2 Cut each slice of bread into 3 strips. Spread the shrimp paste thickly on one side of each strip of bread, then sprinkle evenly with sesame seeds. Press the seeds down firmly, then chill in the refrigerator for about 30 minutes, to firm them up.
3 Heat the oil in a wok until very hot but not smoking. Deep-fry the toasts a few at a time, paste-side down, for 2–3 minutes or until golden. Lift them out with a slotted spoon and drain, paste-side up, on paper towels. Serve hot, with soy sauce for dipping.

Makes 36
Preparation time: 30 minutes, plus chilling
Cooking time: 10–15 minutes

Bean Curd Soup

Also called tofu, bean curd comes from puréed, processed soybeans. It is inexpensive yet very nutritious, high in protein and low in fat. The Chinese use it a lot in their everyday cooking.

1 Bring the stock to a boil in a large saucepan. Add the ginger, carrot, and frozen peas, stir well, then cover and simmer for 5 minutes.

2 Blend the cornstarch to a paste with a little cold water, then pour into the soup and stir to mix. Simmer, stirring, for 1–2 minutes until the soup thickens.

3 Add the soy sauce and stir well, then add the bean curd and heat through for about 1 minute. Taste and add salt and pepper, plus more soy sauce if you like. Serve piping hot, garnished with cilantro.

Cook's Notes

This is an excellent soup for vegetarians as part of a Chinese meal. For a more substantial soup to serve as a main meal, simply double the quantity of carrot and bean curd. Nonvegetarians can add about ¼ lb. peeled cooked shrimp, crabmeat, or thin strips of cooked chicken with the bean curd in step 3.

Serves 4
Preparation time: 15 minutes
Cooking time: about 15 minutes

3½ cups Chicken Stock (see p. 14)
1 inch piece of fresh ginger, peeled and cut into very thin sticks
1 medium carrot cut into matchsticks
2 oz. frozen peas
1 tablespoon cornstarch
2 tablespoons soy sauce, or more to taste
5 oz. firm bean curd (tofu), drained and cut into very thin strips
salt and pepper
cilantro, to garnish

Eight Treasure Soup

4 cups Chicken Stock (see p.14)
  or water
2 oz. frozen peas
2 oz. frozen corn
1 small boneless, skinless chicken
  breast, weighing about 3½ oz.,
  cut into very thin strips
3 oz. fresh shiitake mushrooms,
  very thinly sliced, with stalks
  removed
3 tablespoons soy sauce, or more
  to taste
2 tablespoons rice wine or dry
  sherry
1 tablespoon cornstarch
2 oz. cooked peeled shrimp,
  defrosted and dried thoroughly
  if frozen
2 oz. cooked ham, thinly sliced
5 oz. firm bean curd (tofu), drained
  and thinly sliced
2 oz. fresh baby spinach leaves,
  trimmed, washed, and very
  finely shredded
salt and pepper

The name "eight treasure" refers to the eight special ingredients used in this soup. In China, the number eight is regarded as providing complete balance and harmony, and eight treasure dishes are made on special occasions, especially at New Year. The dish will look particularly attractive if you leave the tails on a few of the shrimp for decoration.

1 Bring the stock or water to a boil in a large saucepan. Add the frozen peas and corn and simmer for 3 minutes. Add the chicken, mushrooms, soy sauce, and rice wine or sherry. Stir well and simmer for 3 minutes.

2 Blend the cornstarch to a paste with a little cold water, then pour it into the soup and stir to mix. Simmer, stirring, for 1–2 minutes until the soup thickens.

3 Turn the heat down to low and add the shrimp, ham, bean curd, and spinach. Simmer for about 2 minutes until the spinach is just wilted, stirring once or twice. Take care to stir gently so that the bean curd does not break up. Taste and add salt and pepper, plus more soy sauce if you like. Serve piping hot.

Cook's Notes
The eight main ingredients can be changed according to personal taste. Pork, crabmeat, dried mushrooms, tomatoes, eggs, and scallions are among the other ingredients that are often used.

Serves 4–6
Preparation time: 15–20 minutes
Cooking time: about 15 minutes

Lamb & Zucchini Fritters

2 large zucchini, each cut
    crossways into 12 rounds
3–4 tablespoons all-purpose flour
2 tablespoons sesame seeds
⅛ lb. ground lamb
1 scallion, finely chopped
1 garlic clove, crushed
about 2 cups peanut oil, for deep-
    frying
2 large eggs, beaten
salt and pepper

1 Coat the zucchini in the flour seasoned with salt and pepper.
2 Put the sesame seeds into a wok and dry-fry over a moderate heat for 1–2 minutes until toasted. Remove and set aside.
3 Mix the ground lamb with the scallion, garlic, and toasted sesame seeds. Press the mixture onto one side of each zucchini round, then coat in more seasoned flour.
4 Heat the oil in a wok until very hot but not smoking. Dip the zucchini rounds into the beaten eggs a few at a time, then deep-fry in batches until golden brown, turning them over once. Lift out of the oil with a slotted spoon, drain on paper towels and keep hot while deep-frying the remainder. Serve immediately.

Makes 24
Preparation time: 20 minutes
Cooking time: about 10 minutes

Red-Oil Dumplings

1 lb all-purpose flour
½ cup boiling water
a little less than ½ cup cold water
1 lb. ground pork
¼ lb. cooked peeled shrimp, very
    finely chopped
1 tablespoon very finely chopped
    fresh ginger root
1 tablespoon very finely chopped
    scallion
1½ teaspoons salt
1 tablespoon soy sauce
1 teaspoon sugar
2 Chinese cabbage leaves, very
    finely chopped
pinch of ground pepper
2 teaspoons sesame oil
DIPPING SAUCE:
1 scallion, finely chopped
1 garlic clove, finely chopped
2 tablespoons peanut butter
2 teaspoons soy sauce
½–1 teaspoon chili oil, to taste
2 teaspoons Chicken Stock
    (see p. 14) or water

1 Sift the flour into a large bowl. Pour in the boiling water; stir to form a firm dough. Leave for a few minutes, then pour in the cold water, reserving 1 tablespoon. Knead well to form a smooth dough.
2 In a bowl, mix together the pork, shrimp, ginger, scallion, salt, soy sauce, sugar, Chinese cabbage, pepper, and sesame oil. Add the remaining 1 tablespoon cold water and beat to form a paste.
3 Form the dough into a long sausage, and divide into 2 inch lengths. Roll each piece into a ball, then roll flat into a small pancake. Place about 1 tablespoon of filling on each pancake and brush the edges with water. Fold over to form half-circles. Pinch the edges firmly to seal.
4 Cook the dumplings in boiling water for 5–6 minutes. Meanwhile, mix together the dipping sauce ingredients. Drain the hot dumplings and serve with the sauce.

Serves 6
Preparation time: 30–40 minutes
Cooking time: 5–6 minutes

Shrimp Puffs

Leaving the tails on these giant shrimp makes it easy to eat them with your fingers. Simply pick them up by their tails and dip them in the sauce. They are ideal for serving with drinks before a Chinese meal.

1 Cut each shrimp in three lengthways without cutting through at the tail end, so that the shrimp remains intact. Rinse under cold running water, then pat thoroughly dry with kitchen paper. Coat in the flour seasoned with salt and pepper.

2 Heat the oil in a wok until very hot but not smoking. Meanwhile, beat the eggs in a bowl with the scallion and five-spice powder.

3 When the oil is hot, dip the shrimp into the egg mixture one at a time. Lift them out with a spoon, making sure there is plenty of egg mixture around each prawn. Lower them gently into the hot oil and deep-fry in batches for 2 minutes or until the shrimp are pink and the coating is crisp and light golden. Lift out the shrimp with a slotted spoon, drain on paper towels, and keep hot while deep-frying the remainder. Serve immediately, with dipping sauces of your choice.

Makes 12
Preparation time: 10–15 minutes
Cooking time: 4–6 minutes

12 raw Mediterranean or large
   shrimp, peeled and deveined,
   tails left on
2 tablespoons all-purpose flour
about 2 cups peanut oil, for deep-
   frying
2 eggs
2 tablespoons very finely chopped
   scallion
½ teaspoon five-spice powder
salt and pepper
sweet and sour sauce and/or soy
   sauce, for dipping

*'Recompense injury with justice, and recompense kindness
with kindness.'*

Confucius

Crispy Lamb with Lettuce

¾ lb. boneless lamb leg steaks or fillet
2 tablespoons soy sauce
I tablespoon rice wine or dry sherry
2 garlic cloves, finely sliced
3 tablespoons cornstarch
about I cup peanut oil, for frying
4 scallions, very finely shredded
8–12 Romaine lettuce leaves, plus extra to serve (optional)
TO SERVE:
plum sauce
¼ red bell pepper, cored, deseeded, and finely *diced* (optional)
¼ red bell pepper, cored, deseeded, and finely *sliced* (optional)

This popular appetizer uses lettuce leaves as wrappers for the lamb. Like pancakes and crispy duck, it should be eaten with your fingers.

1 Cut the lamb across the grain into strips about 2 inches long and ½ inch thick.

2 Put the soy sauce, rice wine or sherry, and the garlic into a nonmetallic dish and stir well to mix. Add the lamb and stir to coat, then cover the dish and leave to marinate in the refrigerator for at least 30 minutes.

3 Sift the cornstarch over the lamb, then stir to mix it in with the meat and marinade. Put the lamb, uncovered, in the refrigerator for about 30 minutes.

4 Heat the oil in a wok until very hot but not smoking. Fry the lamb in about 4 batches for about 3 minutes per batch until crisp and browned. Lift the pieces of lamb out with a slotted spoon and set aside to drain on paper towels.

5 To serve, arrange the lamb, lettuce, and scallions in separate dishes and let each person make their own package. The plum sauce should be spooned onto the lettuce, then the lamb and scallions sprinkled on top, and the lettuce wrapped around them. Garnish with finely diced red pepper, and serve with more lettuce and some finely sliced red pepper if liked.

Cook's Notes

Marinating the lamb helps give it more flavor, while chilling it after coating it in cornstarch helps to make it crispy, but if you are in a hurry you can dispense with both marinating and chilling.

Don't overcrowd the wok when deep-frying. This will lower the temperature of the oil and the lamb will not become crisp.

You can buy bottles of ready-made plum sauce in Chinese supermarkets. It is sweet and sticky, and really delicious with the garlicky lamb.

Serves 4–6

Preparation time: 10 minutes, plus marinating and chilling
Cooking time: about 15 minutes

Spring Rolls

1 pkge. spring roll wrappers or
    4 sheets frozen phyllo pastry,
    defrosted
beaten egg, for sealing
about 2 cups peanut oil, for deep-
    frying
FILLING:
1 tablespoon peanut oil
1 red bell pepper, cored, deseeded,
    and finely chopped
4 scallions, finely chopped
1 inch piece of fresh ginger, peeled
    and finely chopped
6 oz. bean sprouts
½ lb. cooked peeled shrimp,
    defrosted and dried thoroughly
    if frozen, coarsely chopped
2 teaspoons soy sauce
2 teaspoons rice wine or dry
    sherry

You can use spring roll wrappers for these spring rolls, but if they are not available, frozen phyllo pastry is just as effective. Defrost the phyllo according to packet instructions, and keep it covered with a damp cloth while using or it will dry out and crack.

1 First make the filling. Heat an empty wok until hot. Add the oil and heat until hot. Add the red bell pepper, scallions, and ginger and stir-fry for 15 seconds. Add the bean sprouts and stir-fry for 1 minute or until just beginning to soften. Add the shrimp, soy sauce, and rice wine or sherry, increase the heat to high and stir-fry for another 2 minutes, tossing the ingredients together until they are quite dry. Tip the mixture into a bowl and leave to cool. Wipe the inside of the wok clean with a paper towel.

2 Cut each sheet of phyllo in half to make 2 equal squares. Divide the filling into 8 equal portions. Place 1 phyllo square on the work surface and spoon 1 portion of the filling along the side nearest to you, about 1½ inches in from the edge. Bring this edge up, then roll it away from you a half turn over the filling. Fold the sides into the center to enclose the filling, then brush all the edges with a little beaten egg. Continue rolling the phyllo around the filling, then place the spring rolls seam-down on a tray or board. Repeat with the remaining phyllo and filling.

3 Heat the oil in a wok until a very hot but not smoking. Deep-fry half of the spring rolls for 4–5 minutes, or until golden brown and crisp on all sides, turning once. Lift out with a slotted spoon and drain on paper towels while deep-frying the remainder. Serve hot.

Cook's Notes
Sheets of phyllo vary according to manufacturer, but most are rectangular, measuring 10–12 x 5–6 inches.

Makes 8
Preparation time: 30 minutes, plus cooling
Cooking time: about 15 minutes

Scrambled Eggs & Ham

1 Heat an empty wok until hot. Add 1 tablespoon of the oil and heat until hot. Add the mushrooms and stir-fry until the juices run, then add the tomatoes, increase the heat to high and stir-fry for 2–3 minutes. Add salt and pepper to taste. Turn the mushrooms and tomatoes into a warmed serving dish, sprinkle with the rice wine, and keep hot. Beat the eggs with salt and pepper to taste.
2 Add the remaining oil to the wok and heat over a moderate heat until hot. Add half of the scallions and stir-fry for 1–2 minutes. Pour in the seasoned eggs and stir-fry for 2–3 minutes until softly scrambled. Fold in the strips of ham and heat through. Spoon the mushroom mixture over the eggs, garnish with the remaining spring onions and sprinkle with the sesame oil. Serve immediately.

Serves 4
Preparation time: 15 minutes
Cooking time: about 15 minutes

3 tablespoons peanut oil
½ lb. button mushrooms, thinly sliced
½ lb. tomatoes, skinned and roughly chopped
2 teaspoons rice wine
5 eggs
1 bunch of scallions, shredded
¼ lb. cooked ham, cut into thin strips
salt and pepper
a few drops of sesame oil, to finish

Deep-fried Wontons

1 First make the filling. Put all the filling ingredients into a bowl with salt and pepper to taste and stir together until evenly mixed.
2 Using a teaspoon, place a little of the filling mixture in the center of each wonton wrapper, brush the edges with a little water, then bring up 2 opposite corners of each wrapper over the filling to form triangular shapes. Bring the 2 bottom corners of each triangle to meet in the center and slightly overlap them to make an envelope shape. Press all the edges firmly to seal.
3 Make the dipping sauce. Put all the ingredients into a small bowl and whisk until the sugar is dissolved.
4 Heat the oil in a wok until hot but not smoking. Deep-fry 4–6 wontons at a time in the hot oil for 2–3 minutes, or until puffed up, golden and crisp. Lift out with a slotted spoon and drain on paper towels. Keep hot while deep-frying the remaining wontons in the same way. Serve the wontons hot, with the dipping sauce.

Makes 24
Preparation time: about 30 minutes
Cooking time: about 20 minutes

24 wonton wrappers, each about 3½ inches square
about 2 cups peanut oil, for deep-frying
FILLING:
6 oz. ground pork
2 scallions, very finely chopped
1 garlic clove, very finely chopped
1 tablespoon rice wine or dry sherry
1 teaspoon superfine sugar
salt and pepper
DIPPING SAUCE:
1 chili, deseeded and very finely chopped
3 tablespoons soy sauce
1 tablespoon rice wine vinegar or white wine or cider vinegar
1 tablespoon sesame oil
2 teaspoons superfine sugar

Potstickers

12–16 round wonton wrappers
2 tablespoons peanut oil
1¾ cups hot Chicken Stock (see page 14)
salt and pepper
soy sauce and/or chili sauce, to serve
FILLING:
8 large raw shrimp, peeled
2 scallions, quartered crossways
1 garlic clove, halved
1 inch piece of fresh ginger, peeled and sliced
1 teaspoon light soy sauce
½ teaspoon rice wine vinegar
pinch of sugar

These little dumplings take their name from the fact that they stick to the pan during cooking. The wonton pastry is first fried, then cooked in stock. The end result is pleasantly chewy and full of flavor.

1 Make the filling. Put all the ingredients in a food processor fitted with a metal blade. Add a pinch each of salt and pepper and process until finely minced. Turn the mixture into a bowl, cover, and chill in the refrigerator for about 30 minutes until firm.
2 Place the wonton wrappers on a work surface. Heap about ½ teaspoon of the filling on each wrapper, placing it slightly off center. Brush all around the edges of the wrappers with water. Fold the plain side of each wrapper over the mound of filling, making three pleats in it as you go. Press the rounded edges to seal in the filling, then pleat all around the rounded edges to make an attractive crimped finish. There is enough filling to make 12 quite plump dumplings, but if you find them difficult to make with so much filling, use less filling and make 16 dumplings.
3 Heat 1 tablespoon of the oil in a wok until hot. Place half of the potstickers flat-side down in the hot oil and fry without disturbing for about 2 minutes until browned on the underside. Pour in half of the stock; this should be enough to just cover the potstickers. Bring to a boil, then lower the heat and simmer for about 10 minutes until the stock has been absorbed into the potstickers. Repeat with the remaining oil, potstickers, and stock. Serve hot, with soy sauce and/or chili sauce for dipping.

Cook's Notes
Wonton wrappers are sold in the refrigerator sections of many supermarkets or of Asian specialty grocers. You can buy both round and square wrappers, but for this recipe you need the round ones, which are about 3 inches in diameter. Made from wheat flour, egg, and water, they are yellowish in color, unlike spring roll wrappers which are pure white.

Makes 12–16
Preparation time: about 30 minutes, plus chilling
Cooking time: about 25 minutes

seafood

With its vast shoreline and endless, winding rivers, China has a dazzling selection of fish and seafood. For generations, fishermen have taken their traditional "junks" out to sea and returned with their intricately woven baskets full of shining prawns, scallops, crabs, and countless varieties of fish. The myriad ways of cooking seafood reflect this natural bounty—they are steamed, stir-fried, simmered, and so on, so their flavors and textures are beautifully preserved and enhanced.

Sweet & Sour Fish

1 egg white
2 teaspoons cornstarch
pinch of salt
1 lb. cod or haddock fillets,
    skinned and cut into 1 inch
    chunks
about 2 cups peanut oil, for deep-
    frying
2 tablespoons finely chopped
    cilantro, to garnish
deep-fried shredded seaweed, to
    serve (optional)
SAUCE:
1 tablespoon cornstarch
½ cup cold fish stock or water
1 tablespoon soy sauce
1 tablespoon rice wine or dry
    sherry
1 tablespoon rice wine vinegar or
    white wine or cider vinegar
1 tablespoon brown sugar
1 tablespoon tomato paste

1 Lightly beat the egg white in a shallow dish with the cornstarch and salt. Add the chunks of fish and turn gently to coat. Set aside.
2 Prepare the sauce. Blend the cornstarch in a small bowl with 2 tablespoons of the stock or water, then add the remaining stock or water and the remaining sauce ingredients. Stir well to combine.
3 Heat the oil in a wok until very hot but not smoking. Deep-fry the fish chunks a few at a time for 2–3 minutes for each batch until golden. Lift out the fish with a slotted spoon and drain on paper towels while deep-frying the remainder.
4 Very carefully pour off all the oil from the wok and wipe the wok clean with a paper towel. Pour the sauce mixture into the wok and bring to the boil over a high heat, stirring constantly until thickened and glossy. Lower the heat, add the fish and simmer gently for 30–60 seconds until heated through. Garnish with finely chopped cilantro and serve immediately, accompanied by deep-fried shredded seaweed, if liked.

Serves 4
Preparation time: 10–15 minutes
Cooking time: 10–15 minutes

'Fuel is not sold in a forest, nor fish on a lake.'

Chinese Proverb

Sichuan Squid

1 lb. prepared squid, quills removed
3 tablespoons peanut oil
1 onion, thinly sliced into rings
1 red bell pepper, cored, deseeded, and thinly sliced into rings
1 yellow or green bell pepper, cored, deseeded, and thinly sliced into rings
1 chili, deseeded and thinly sliced into rings
SAUCE:
1 tablespoon cornstarch
4 tablespoons cold water
2 garlic cloves, crushed
3 tablespoons soy sauce
2 tablespoons chili sauce
1 teaspoon sugar

Prepared squid is available at the fresh fish counters of large supermarkets. It is very convenient to buy it in this way as whole fresh squid with their ink sacks intact are time consuming and messy to handle. Choose the smallest squid available, as these will be the most tender, but in any case never overcook squid or it will become tough and chewy.

1 Slice the squid neatly into ½ inch thick rings. Leave the tentacles whole or chop them, depending on their size. Blanch the squid in boiling water for 30 seconds, drain, then rinse under cold water and pat dry. Set aside.
2 Prepare the sauce. Mix the cornstarch to a paste with the water, then stir in the garlic, soy sauce, chili sauce, and sugar. Set aside.
3 Heat an empty wok until hot. Add 2 tablespoons of the oil and heat until hot. Add the onion, peppers, and chili and stir-fry over a moderate heat for 5 minutes or until the peppers are tender. Transfer the pepper mixture to a plate with a slotted spoon.
4 Add the remaining oil to the wok and heat until hot. Add the squid and stir-fry for 2–3 minutes or until just tender. Remove with a slotted spoon and set aside with the vegetables.
5 Stir the sauce to mix, then pour it into the wok. Increase the heat to high and stir vigorously until boiling. Return the squid, the vegetables, and their juices to the wok and toss until coated in the sauce and piping hot. Serve immediately.

Serves 3–4
Preparation time: 20 minutes
Cooking time: about 15 minutes

'Men's natures are alike; it is their habits that carry them far apart.'

Confucius

Stir-fried Shrimp with Bean Curd

Firm bean curd (tofu) can be bought loose in Asian markets, or in packages at supermarkets and health food shops. Made from puréed processed soybeans, it is high in protein yet low in fat.

about 1 cup peanut oil, for frying
½ lb. firm bean curd (tofu), drained, dried and cut into cubes
½ lb. cooked peeled shrimp, defrosted and dried thoroughly if frozen
SAUCE:
2 tablespoons soy sauce
2 tablespoons rice wine or dry sherry
1 tablespoon lemon juice
1 teaspoon sugar
2 teaspoons cornstarch
just under ½ cup cold fish stock or water

1 First prepare the sauce. Put the soy sauce, rice wine or sherry, and the lemon juice into a small bowl, add the sugar and cornstarch, and stir well to mix. Stir in the stock or water. Set aside.

2 Heat the oil in a wok until very hot but not smoking. Add the bean curd and pan-fry for 2–3 minutes or until it is golden on all sides, taking care not to let it break up. Lift out with a slotted spoon, drain on paper towels, and keep warm.

3 Very carefully pour off all but about 1 tablespoon of oil from the wok. Add the shrimp, increase the heat to high and stir-fry for 1–2 minutes. Stir the sauce to mix, then pour it into the wok. Bring to a boil, stirring, then add the bean curd and stir gently to combine with the shrimp and coat in the sauce. Serve immediately.

Serves 3–4
Preparation time: 10 minutes
Cooking time: about 10 minutes

Sweet Garlic Shrimp

2 tablespoons peanut oil
4 garlic cloves, crushed
1 inch piece of fresh ginger, peeled and cut into julienne strips
1–2 teaspoons chili powder, to taste
1 lb. cooked peeled shrimp, defrosted and dried thoroughly if frozen
SAUCE:
2 teaspoons cornstarch
4 tablespoons cold fish stock or water
4 tablespoons soy sauce
2 tablespoons honey

1 First prepare the sauce. Mix the cornstarch to a paste with a little of the stock or water, then stir in the remaining stock or water, the soy sauce, and honey. Set aside.

2 Heat an empty wok until hot. Add the oil and heat until hot. Add the garlic, ginger, and chili powder and stir-fry over a low heat for 2–3 minutes or until softened, taking care not to let the ingredients brown. Add the shrimp, increase the heat to high and stir-fry for 1–2 minutes, just until they are hot.

3 Stir the sauce, then pour it over the shrimp. Increase the heat to high and toss just until the shrimp are coated in the sauce. Serve immediately.

Serves 3–4
Preparation time: 10 minutes
Cooking time: about 10 minutes

Sea-spiced Shrimp

6 dried shiitake mushrooms
about ½ cup hot water
2 tablespoons peanut oil
1 red bell pepper, cored, deseeded,
    and diced
2 garlic cloves, finely chopped
1 red chili, deseeded and finely
    chopped
12–16 raw tiger shrimp, peeled
    and deveined
1 cup hot Chicken Stock (p. 14)
2 tablespoons oyster sauce
3½ oz. canned water chestnuts,
    drained and sliced
2 teaspoons cornstarch
salt and pepper
1 tablespoon finely chopped
    cilantro, to garnish (optional)

Oyster sauce accentuates the fishy flavor of this spicy hot dish, while the water chestnuts provide a crisp contrast to the soft texture of the shrimp.

1 Soak the dried mushrooms in the hot water for 35–40 minutes. Drain the mushrooms in a sieve over a bowl and reserve the soaking water. Cut the mushroom caps into small square shapes, discarding any hard stalks.
2 Heat an empty wok until hot. Add the oil and heat until hot, then add the red bell pepper, mushrooms, garlic, and chili and stir-fry over a moderate heat for 2–3 minutes.
3 Add the shrimp and stir-fry for 1–2 minutes until they are just turning pink, then pour in the stock, the oyster sauce, and water chestnuts. Stir well, then let the stock simmer gently for 1–2 minutes.
4 Blend the cornstarch to a paste with a little cold water, pour it into the wok, and stir to mix. Simmer, stirring, for 1–2 minutes until the sauce thickens, then taste for seasoning and adjust if necessary. Serve immediately, garnished with cilantro if you like.

Cook's Notes
Raw tiger shrimp are the best type of shrimp for Chinese stir-fries because they are large and juicy, but if you can't get them you can use other shrimp instead. If you use cooked peeled shrimp, you will need about ½ lb. and they should be added with the water chestnuts in step 3. If they are frozen, make sure to defrost and dry them thoroughly before use.

Serves 3–4
Preparation time: 15 minutes, plus soaking
Cooking time: about 10 minutes

Scallops with Lemon & Ginger

8 fresh shelled scallops, with corals
3 tablespoons peanut oil
½ bunch of scallions, thinly sliced
  on the diagonal
3 tablespoons lemon juice
2 tablespoons rice wine or dry
  sherry
2 pieces of Chinese stem ginger
  with I tablespoon syrup,
  chopped
salt and pepper
lemon slices or segments, to
  garnish

1 Slice the scallops thickly. Detach the corals and keep them whole.
2 Heat an empty wok until hot. Add 2 tablespoons of the oil and heat until hot. Add the scallops and stir-fry over a moderate heat for 3 minutes, then transfer them to a plate with a slotted spoon.
3 Heat the remaining oil in the wok until hot. Add the scallions and stir-fry for a few seconds, then add the lemon juice and rice wine or sherry and bring to a boil. Stir in the stem ginger and about 1 tablespoon of the syrup.
4 Return the scallops and their juices to the wok and toss quickly over a high heat until heated through. Add the reserved corals and stir-fry for 30 seconds. Add salt and pepper to taste and serve immediately, garnished with lemon.

Serves 2–4
Preparation time: 10 minutes
Cooking time: 10 minutes

Quick-fried Fish in Yellow Bean Sauce

I lb. monkfish, skinned and cut
  into chunky pieces
I tablespoon peanut oil
MARINADE:
4 tablespoons cold fish stock
3 tablespoons soy sauce
2 tablespoons yellow bean sauce
I tablespoon rice wine or dry
  sherry
I teaspoon sugar

Yellow bean sauce is traditional with chicken in Chinese stir-fries, but it goes equally well with monkfish, as this recipe illustrates. The jars of yellow bean sauce sold in large supermarkets have an excellent flavor and are extremely useful for giving stir-fries an instant Chinese flavor, so it is well worth keeping a jar in the refrigerator.

1 First make the marinade. Mix all the ingredients in a shallow dish, add the monkfish and turn gently to coat. Cover and leave to marinate in the refrigerator for 1–2 hours, turning the fish occasionally.
2 Heat an empty wok until hot. Add the oil and heat until hot. Add the fish and its marinade and stir-fry over a high heat for 4–5 minutes or until the fish is cooked. Serve immediately.

Serves 3–4
Preparation time: 5 minutes, plus marinating
Cooking time: 5–6 minutes

Quick-fried Flounder & Scallions

1 Blend the sauce ingredients together in a small bowl.
2 Lightly beat the egg white in a shallow dish with the cornstarch, sesame seeds, and salt. Add the strips of flounder; turn gently to coat.
3 Heat the oil in a wok until very hot but not smoking. Pan-fry the flounder a few pieces at a time for about 2 minutes for each batch or until golden. Lift the flounder out with a slotted spoon and drain on paper towels. Keep the fish hot in a serving dish while cooking the remainder.
4 Very carefully pour off all but about 1 tablespoon of the oil from the wok. Add the scallions, ginger, and garlic and stir-fry for 30 seconds, then pour in the sauce ingredients and bring to a boil over a high heat, stirring constantly. Pour the sauce over the fish and serve immediately.

Serves 2–3
Preparation time: 10–15 minutes
Cooking time: 10 minutes

1 egg white
2 teaspoons cornstarch
2 teaspoons sesame seeds
pinch of salt
¾ lb. flounder fillets, cut into thin
    strips 1½ inches long
about ⅓ cup peanut oil
4 scallions, thinly sliced on the
    diagonal
1 inch piece of fresh ginger, peeled
    and chopped
1 garlic clove, crushed
SAUCE:
2 tablespoons soy sauce
1 tablespoon rice wine or dry
    sherry
1 tablespoon lemon juice
1 teaspoon brown sugar
good pinch of five-spice powder

Steamed Whole Fish

2 whole sea bass, each weighing
    about 1 lb., gutted and trimmed
    with heads and tails left on
2 inch piece of fresh ginger, peeled
    and very thinly sliced
6 scallions, sliced crossways into
    very thin rings
4 garlic cloves, finely sliced
6 teaspoons sesame oil
3 heaping tablespoons canned
    salted black beans, rinsed
3 tablespoons peanut oil
2 tablespoons rice wine or dry
    sherry
2–3 tablespoons chopped cilantro,
    to garnish
bean thread noodles, to serve

A whole fish is a symbol of prosperity in China, which is why you so often see whole fish served on large platters or trays at banquets. The head and tail are always left on the fish, and the head should face toward the guest of honor.

1 Fill a large wok about one-third full with cold water, then place a large bamboo steamer in the wok, making sure that it does not touch the water. Bring the water to a boil over a moderate heat.

2 Meanwhile, with a cleaver or sharp knife, make diagonal slashes on each side of the fish, working right down to the bones. Place the two fish head-to-tail on a plate that will just fit inside the steamer. Insert the slices of ginger inside the fish and in the diagonal slashes, then sprinkle about half of the scallions and garlic inside and over the fish. Drizzle each fish with 2 teaspoons of the sesame oil.

3 Put the plate of fish inside the steamer and cover with the lid. Steam over a high heat for 8 minutes, without lifting the lid.

4 Meanwhile, mash about two-thirds of the black beans, leaving the remainder whole. Heat the remaining sesame oil and the peanut oil in a small wok or saucepan. Add the remaining scallions and garlic, the mashed and whole black beans, and the rice wine or sherry to the wok. Stir-fry over a high heat for a few minutes until sizzling.

5 Transfer the fish to a warmed serving platter. Pour any fish juices from the cooking plate into the black bean sauce, then spoon the sauce over the fish. Serve immediately with bean thread noodles, garnished with cilantro.

Cook's Notes

Unless you actually buy your bamboo steamer and wok together, you can't be sure that their sizes are a good match for each other. The steamer should just fit inside the rim of the wok so that it does not actually come into contact with the water. If the diameter of the steamer is much smaller than the wok, the steamer will fit too low down. Fortunately, this can easily be remedied by standing the steamer on a metal trivet.

Serves 2–4

Preparation time: 20 minutes
Cooking time: about 10 minutes

Shanghai Smoked Fish

¼ lb. flounder fillets, halved lengthwise
a scant ½ cup boiling water
2 egg whites
4 teaspoons cornstarch
¾ cup peanut oil, for frying
MARINADE:
1 inch piece of fresh ginger, peeled and finely chopped
2 tablespoons rice wine or dry sherry
2 tablespoons soy sauce
2 teaspoons dark brown sugar
½ teaspoon five-spice powder
¼ teaspoon salt

This dish is so called because it has the appearance and flavor of smoked fish, although it is not smoked at all.

1 First make the marinade. Whisk the ginger in a shallow dish with the rice wine or sherry, soy sauce, sugar, five-spice powder, and salt. Add the pieces of fish and spoon the marinade over them. Cover and leave to marinate in the refrigerator for 1–2 hours, spooning the marinade over the fish occasionally.
2 When you are ready to cook, carefully lift the pieces of fish out of the marinade with a slotted spatula and pat dry with paper towels.
3 Pour the marinade into the wok, add the boiling water and bring to a boil, stirring. Simmer for about 10 minutes until thickened, stirring frequently. Strain into a bowl and keep warm. Wipe the wok clean with paper towels.
4 Lightly beat the egg whites in a shallow dish with the cornstarch. Add the pieces of flounder and turn gently to coat. Heat the oil in the wok until very hot but not smoking. Carefully lower a few pieces of the flounder, skin-side up, into the wok. Pan-fry each batch for 4–5 minutes, turning them over once. Lift out with a slotted spoon and drain on paper towels while cooking the remainder. Arrange the fish on a serving platter, pour the warm marinade over, and leave to cool. Serve at room temperature.

Serves 4
Preparation time: 10 minutes, plus marinating and cooling
Cooking time: 20–25 minutes

'Govern a family as you would cook a small fish – very gently.'

Chinese Proverb

Fish Balls with Sweet & Sour Sauce

1 Put the fish into a food processor, add the cilantro, soy sauce, egg white, cornstarch, and pepper to taste, then work until smooth and evenly mixed.

2 Turn the mixture into a bowl, then, with hands dipped in cold water, shape into about 36 small balls. Place the fish balls on a tray and chill in the refrigerator for about 30 minutes or until firm.

3 Meanwhile, prepare the sauce. Blend the cornstarch to a paste with the cold water, then stir in the remaining sauce ingredients.

4 Pour the fish stock into the wok, add the soy sauce and scallions, and bring to the boil over a moderate heat. Lower the heat to a gentle simmer and drop in the fish balls. Poach for 6 minutes, then lift out with a slotted spoon and keep hot.

5 Pour off all but about ½ cup of stock from the wok. Stir the sauce, then pour it into the wok. Increase the heat to high and boil until thickened, stirring all the time. Return the fish balls to the wok and shake to coat them in the sauce. Serve hot, sprinkled with chopped cilantro.

Serves 4–6
Preparation time: 20 minutes, plus chilling
Cooking time: about 20 minutes

1 lb. white fish fillets, skinned and
  roughly chopped
1 tablespoon finely chopped
  cilantro
2 teaspoons soy sauce
1 egg white
1 tablespoon cornstarch
pepper
3 cups hot fish stock
2 tablespoons soy sauce
2 scallions, roughly chopped
chopped cilantro, to garnish
SAUCE:
2 teaspoons cornstarch
2 tablespoons cold water
2 tablespoons soy sauce
2 tablespoons rice wine or dry
  sherry
1 tablespoon rice wine vinegar or
  white wine vinegar or cider
  vinegar
2 teaspoons tomato purée
2 teaspoons brown sugar

Fish with Creamy Rice

1 cup long-grain rice
5½ cups Chicken Stock (see p. 14)
3 tablespoons peanut oil
1 tablespoon finely chopped garlic
1 lb. cod fillet, thinly sliced
2 tablespoons soy sauce
1 teaspoon pepper
TO GARNISH:
2 scallions, shredded
2 celery sticks, very finely chopped

1 Rinse the rice several times in a sieve under cold running water, then drain well.

2 Bring 2 cups of the stock to a boil in a large saucepan. Add the rice, then cook for 15–20 minutes over a low heat, stirring from time to time. The rice should absorb most of the stock. Add the remaining stock, bring it back to a boil, then remove the pan from the heat and cover with a lid.

3 Heat an empty wok until hot. Add the oil and heat until hot, then add the garlic and stir-fry until just golden. With a slotted spoon, transfer the garlic to a small plate.

4 Add the cod to the oil remaining in the wok and stir-fry for 4–6 minutes. As soon as it is cooked, add the cod to the rice together with the soy sauce and pepper. Mix well and transfer to a warmed serving dish. Garnish with the scallions, celery, and fried garlic and serve immediately.

Serves 4
Preparation time: 10 minutes
Cooking time: 25–30 minutes

Fish Fillets in Hot Sauce

Because of its delicate texture, white fish has a tendency to break up during stir-frying. This method of coating strips of fish in egg white and cornstarch and then deep-frying them in hot oil is good for holding the pieces of fish together. The batter is light and delicate, and the hot sauce provides a good, sharp contrast of flavors.

1 Lightly beat the egg white in a shallow dish, add the strips of fish and turn to coat. Spread the cornstarch on a board or plate, then dip the fish in the cornstarch until lightly coated on all sides.

2 Heat the oil in a wok until very hot but not smoking. Deep-fry the fish in 4–6 batches for about 2 minutes for each batch until crisp and light golden. Lift out with a slotted spoon and drain on paper towels. Very carefully pour off all the hot oil from the wok and wipe the wok clean with a paper towel.

3 Add all the sauce ingredients to the wok, place over a moderate heat and bring to the boil, stirring. Simmer until the sauce is reduced slightly, then lower the heat, return the fish to the wok and heat through for 1 minute. Serve immediately.

Cook's Notes
If you prefer not to deep-fry the fish, then it is best to use a firm-fleshed fish such as monkfish, in which case it need not be coated in batter and can simply be stir-fried in a few tablespoons of hot oil.

Serves 3–4
Preparation time: 10 minutes
Cooking time: about 15 minutes

1 egg white
1 lb. white fish fillets, preferably flounder, cut into chunky strips
2 tablespoons cornstarch
about 2 cups peanut oil, for deep-frying
SAUCE:
½ cup fish stock
2 tablespoons soy sauce
2 tablespoons chili sauce
1 tablespoon lemon juice
1 tablespoon tomato purée
2 teaspoons brown sugar

Fish in Wine Sauce

about ¾ lb. white fish fillets,
    skinned
1 egg white
2 garlic cloves, finely chopped
1 tablespoon cornstarch
about 1 cup peanut oil, for frying
salt and pepper
a few drops chili oil, to serve
1 tablespoon chopped cilantro
    leaves, to garnish
WINE SAUCE:
1 cup hot Chicken Stock
    (see page 14)
6 tablespoons rice wine
1 tablespoon cornstarch
½ teaspoon sugar, or more to taste
2 tablespoons chopped cilantro

This delicately flavored dish is a classic that is not widely known. This is a pity because it is delicious and easy to make, ideal for the home cook.

1 Cut the fish into bite-sized pieces. Put the egg white and garlic into a bowl with salt and pepper to taste and whisk with a fork until frothy. Sift in the cornstarch and whisk to mix, then add the fish and stir until coated.

2 Heat the oil in a wok until very hot but not smoking. Deep-fry the fish in 4–6 batches for about 2 minutes for each batch until crisp and light golden. Lift out with a slotted spoon and drain on paper towels. Very carefully pour off all the hot oil from the wok and wipe the wok clean with paper towels.

3 Make the sauce. Pour the stock and rice wine into the wok and bring to the boil over a high heat. Blend the cornstarch to a paste with a little cold water, then pour it into the wok and stir to mix. Simmer, stirring, for 2 minutes until thickened.

4 Add the sugar and stir to dissolve, then stir in the chopped cilantro. Return the fish to the wok. Stir the fish very gently to coat it in the sauce and heat through for 1–2 minutes, then taste for seasoning and add more sugar if liked. Serve very hot with a few drops of chili oil and garnished with cilantro leaves.

Cook's Notes

You can use any white fish you like. Lemon sole and flounder are often used, but for a more robust texture you could try sea bass fillets, which are available at some of the large supermarkets with fresh fish counters.

Look for Shaoxing or Shaohsing rice wine in Chinese supermarkets. It is reputed to be the best and is well worth buying for a dish like this in which the wine is one of the main flavorings. It has a rich, mellow flavor and is suitable for both drinking and cooking. If stored in a cool place, it will keep for months.

Serves 4
Preparation time: 15 minutes
Cooking time: about 20 minutes

chicken
& duck

What could bring more delight to the Chinese heart than a succulent dish of aromatic, crispy duck or a plate of sizzling chicken in garlic sauce? Throughout China, the poultry yard has been a crucial part of the family's sustenance, valued not only for meat and eggs for the larder, but also for supplies of soft warm feathers and down to fill pillows and featherbeds—essential for warmth during the fiercely cold winters.

Chicken with Sizzling Garlic Sauce

2 boneless, skinless chicken
    breasts, total weight 8–10 oz.
1 small egg
2 garlic cloves, crushed
about 4 tablespoons cornstarch
about ³/₄ cup peanut oil, for frying
salt and pepper
a few drops of chili oil (optional),
    to serve
SAUCE:
4 scallions (white part only), finely
    shredded
2 garlic cloves, finely chopped
1 scant cup hot Chicken Stock
    (see page 14)
4 tablespoons rice wine or dry
    sherry
1 teaspoon cornstarch
TO GARNISH:
½ tablespoon finely chopped red
    bell pepper
½ tablespoon finely chopped green
    bell pepper
1 tablespoon chopped cilantro

This is a simple dish with relatively few ingredients, but the garlic gives it a good flavor. It is pale in color, so if you are going to serve it as part of a Chinese meal, the other dishes should be bright and colorful to achieve the correct balance.

1 Put the chicken breasts between plastic wrap and pound them with the base of a saucepan to flatten them. Remove the plastic wrap and cut the chicken into strips about 1 inch wide.
2 Beat the egg in a bowl with the crushed garlic and plenty of salt and pepper. Dip the chicken strips in the egg mixture, then place them in a single layer on a plate and dredge them with cornstarch. Place the plate in the refrigerator for 30 minutes to 1 hour, or longer if you have the time.
3 Heat the oil in a wok until very hot but not smoking. Immerse the chicken pieces in the hot oil one at a time until there are enough to fit in the pan in a single layer without overcrowding. Fry for about 3 minutes or until the chicken is golden, turning once. Remove with a slotted spoon and keep hot in a warmed bowl. Repeat with the remaining chicken.
4 Very carefully pour off all but about 1 teaspoon of the hot oil from the wok. Return the wok to a low heat and make the sauce. Put the spring onions, chopped garlic, stock, and rice wine or sherry in the wok. Increase the heat to high and bring to a boil, stirring.
5 Blend the cornstarch to a paste with a little cold water, then pour it into the wok and stir to mix. Simmer, stirring, for 1–2 minutes until the sauce thickens, then pour it over the chicken. Garnish with red and green bell pepper and chopped cilantro and sprinkle with a few drops of chili oil, if desired. Serve immediately.

Serves 2–4
Preparation time: 10–15 minutes, plus chilling
Cooking time: 15–20 minutes

Chairman Mao's Chicken

2 egg whites
2 tablespoons cornstarch
4 boneless, skinless chicken
    breasts, each weighing about
    5 oz., cut into thin strips against
    the grain
about 2 cups peanut oil, for deep-
    frying
3 carrots, cut into julienne strips
3 celery sticks, thinly sliced on the
    diagonal
3 scallions, thinly sliced on the
    diagonal
1 inch piece of fresh ginger, peeled
    and cut into julienne strips
2 garlic cloves, finely chopped
2 chilies, deseeded and finely
    chopped
½ cup hot Chicken Stock (see
    page 14) or water
2 tablespoons chili sauce
1 tablespoon rice wine or dry
    sherry
1 teaspoon brown sugar
¼ teaspoon salt

Chairman Mao was very fond of hot and spicy food. This recipe uses fresh chilies and chili sauce, and so is named after him. For a really hot flavor, include some, or all, of the seeds from the chilies.

1 Lightly beat the egg whites in a shallow dish with the cornstarch Add the chicken and turn to coat.
2 Heat the oil in a wok until very hot but not smoking. One at a time, lift the chicken strips out of the egg mixture with a fork and drop them into the hot oil. Deep-fry in batches for 3–4 minutes or until golden and tender. Lift out with a slotted spoon and drain on paper towels while deep-frying the remainder.
3 Very carefully pour off all but about 2 tablespoons of oil from the wok. Add all the vegetables, the ginger, garlic, and chilies and stir-fry over a moderate heat for 2–3 minutes, then add the chicken stock or water, the chili sauce, rice wine or sherry, sugar, and salt. Stir for 2 minutes or until the carrots are just tender.
4 Return the chicken to the wok and stir for 1–2 minutes or until all the ingredients are well combined and piping hot. Serve immediately.

Serves 3–4
Preparation time: 20 minutes
Cooking time: about 20 minutes

'Chi Wen Teu always thought three times before taking action. Twice would have been quite enough.'

Confucius

Chicken Chop Suey

The name chop suey comes from the Chinese word zasui *meaning mixed bits. The choice of meat and vegetables for a chop suey can vary according to what is available, making it the ideal dish for using up leftovers and vegetables from the freezer. Try to use at least one seasonal vegetable to give the chop suey a fresh flavor.*

1 First prepare the sauce. Blend the cornstarch to a thin paste with the cold water, then stir in the soy sauce, rice wine or sherry, vinegar, and sugar.

2 Heat an empty wok until hot. Add the oil and heat until hot. Add the onion and carrots and stir-fry over a moderate heat for 2 minutes, then add the green bell pepper and stir-fry for 2 minutes. Add the peas and corn, toss well to mix, then pour in the stock and bring to a boil, stirring. Simmer for 3–4 minutes, stirring.

3 Stir the sauce to mix, then pour it into the wok and increase the heat to high. Stir constantly until thickened.

4 Add the chicken and bean sprouts and toss for about 2 minutes or until evenly combined and piping hot. Add pepper to taste and serve immediately.

Serves 3–4
Preparation time: 20 minutes
Cooking time: about 10 minutes

3 tablespoons peanut oil
I small onion, finely chopped
3 carrots, cut into julienne strips
I green bell pepper, cored, deseeded, and cut into julienne strips
I cup frozen peas
¾ cup frozen corn
½ cup hot Chicken Stock (see page 14)
½–¾ lb. boneless cooked chicken meat, skinned and cut into strips
3 oz. bean sprouts
pepper
SAUCE:
2 teaspoons cornstarch
4 tablespoons water
3 tablespoons soy sauce
2 tablespoons rice wine or dry sherry
I tablespoon rice wine vinegar or white wine or cider vinegar
2 teaspoons brown sugar

Chicken in Chili & Black Bean Sauce

2 boneless, skinless chicken
    breasts, total weight 8–10 oz.
1 egg white
1 tablespoon cornstarch
about 1 cup peanut oil, for frying
1 green bell pepper, cored,
    deseeded and cut lengthways
    into thin strips
1 green chili, deseeded and very
    finely shredded
4 garlic cloves, cut into very thin
    strips
4 scallions, shredded
4 tablespoons black bean sauce
1 cup hot Chicken Stock (see
    page 14)
salt and pepper
boiled and drained egg noodles,
    to serve
1–2 heaped tablespoons canned
    salted black beans, rinsed,
    to garnish

Chicken with green pepper, chili, garlic, and black beans is a classic combination. It is one of the most delicious of Chinese stir-fries, and this version is very easy to make.

1 Cut the chicken into thin strips, working diagonally against the grain. Put the egg white into a bowl with salt and pepper to taste and whisk with a fork until frothy. Sift in the cornstarch and whisk to mix, then add the chicken and stir until coated.

2 Heat the oil in a wok until very hot but not smoking. Add about one-quarter of the chicken strips and stir them around so that they separate. Pan-fry for 30–60 seconds until the chicken turns white on all sides. Lift out with a slotted spoon and drain on paper towels. Repeat with the remaining chicken. Very carefully pour off all but about 1 tablespoon of the hot oil from the wok.

3 Return the wok to a low heat and add the green bell pepper, chili, garlic, and about half of the scallions. Stir-fry for a few minutes until the pepper begins to soften, then add the black bean sauce and stir to mix. Pour in the stock, increase the heat to high, and bring to a boil, stirring.

4 Put the chicken into the sauce and cook over a moderate to high heat, stirring frequently, for 5 minutes. Taste for seasoning. Serve hot with egg noodles, garnished with the remaining scallions and the black beans.

Cook's Notes

Black bean sauce is available in small bottles at most supermarkets. It is excellent for making quick stir-fries.

The technique of coating and frying the chicken at the beginning of this recipe is called "velveting" or "going through the oil." It is most often used with chicken and fish to protect their delicate flesh. The food has a perfect finish—slightly crisp on the outside and meltingly tender inside. You can reuse the oil once or twice more, so don't throw it away after pouring it out of the wok at the end of step 2. Let it go cold, then strain it and pour it into a bottle.

Serves 2–4
Preparation time: 10–15 minutes
Cooking time: about 20 minutes

Chicken with Cashews

2 tablespoons peanut oil
4 boneless, skinless chicken
    breasts, each weighing about
    5 oz., cut into thin strips against
    the grain
1 bunch of scallions, thinly sliced
    on the diagonal
2 garlic cloves, crushed
1–1½ cups cashews
pepper
boiled or steamed rice, to serve
SAUCE:
2 teaspoons cornstarch
6 tablespoons Chicken Stock
    (see page 14) or water
3 tablespoons soy sauce
2 tablespoons rice wine or dry
    sherry
2 teaspoons brown sugar

1 First prepare the sauce. Blend the cornstarch to a paste with 1 tablespoon of the stock or water, then stir in the remaining stock or water, the soy sauce, rice wine, or sherry and sugar.
2 Heat an empty wok until hot. Add the oil and heat until hot. Add the chicken strips and stir-fry over a high heat for 3–4 minutes or until lightly colored on all sides. Add the scallions and garlic and stir-fry for 1 minute.
3 Stir the sauce, then pour it into the wok and bring to a boil, stirring. Add the cashews and mix them with the chicken and scallions. Season with pepper. Serve hot, with steamed rice.

Serves 3–4
Preparation time: 10 minutes
Cooking time: 5–6 minutes

Sesame Chicken

2 egg whites
2 tablespoons cornstarch
2 tablespoons sesame seeds
¼ teaspoon salt
4 boneless, skinless chicken
    breasts, each weighing about
    5 oz., cut into thin strips against
    the grain
about 1 cup peanut oil, for frying
2 teaspoons sesame oil
SAUCE:
2 tablespoons soy sauce
2 tablespoons rice wine or dry
    sherry
1 tablespoon rice wine vinegar or
    white wine or cider vinegar
2 teaspoons brown sugar
½ teaspoon chili powder, or
    to taste

This dish is simple and quick. Serve it with a colorful and crunchy mixed vegetable stir-fry.

1 Prepare the sauce. Mix all the ingredients together in a small bowl.
2 Lightly beat the egg whites in a shallow dish with the cornstarch, sesame seeds, and salt. Add the strips of chicken and turn to coat.
3 Heat the peanut oil in a wok until very hot but not smoking. One at a time, lift the strips of chicken out of the egg white mixture with a fork and drop them into the hot oil. Pan-fry the chicken in batches for about 3–4 minutes at a time until golden. Lift out with a slotted spoon and drain on paper towels.
4 Very carefully pour off all the oil from the wok. Wipe the wok clean with paper towels. Return the wok to a moderate heat, pour in the sauce and stir until sizzling. Return the chicken to the wok and toss for 1–2 minutes or until evenly coated in the sauce. Sprinkle with the sesame oil and serve immediately.

Serves 3–4
Preparation time: 10 minutes
Cooking time: about 15 minutes

Lemon Chicken

1 First prepare the sauce. Blend the cornstarch to a thin paste with the stock or water, then stir in the remaining sauce ingredients.
2 Lightly beat the egg white in a shallow dish with the cornstarch and salt. Add the strips of chicken and turn to coat.
3 Heat the oil in a wok until very hot but not smoking. One at a time, lift the strips of chicken out of the egg white mixture with a fork and drop them into the hot oil. Pan-fry in batches for about 3–4 minutes at a time until golden. Lift out with a slotted spoon and drain on paper towels.
4 Very carefully pour off all but about 1 tablespoon of oil from the wok. Add the scallions and garlic and stir-fry over a moderate heat for 30 seconds. Stir the sauce to mix, pour it into the wok, increase the heat to high and bring to the boil, stirring constantly.
5 Return the chicken to the wok and stir-fry for 1–2 minutes or until evenly coated in the sauce. Serve immediately, garnished with lemon slices.

Serves 2
Preparation time: 10 minutes
Cooking time: about 15 minutes

1 egg white
2 teaspoons cornstarch
pinch of salt
2 boneless, skinless chicken
    breasts, each weighing about
    5 oz., cut into thin strips against
    the grain
about 1 cup peanut oil, for frying
½ bunch of scallions, shredded
1 garlic clove, crushed
lemon slices, to garnish
SAUCE:
2 teaspoons cornstarch
4 tablespoons Chicken Stock
    (see page 14) or water
finely grated rind of ½ lemon
2 tablespoons lemon juice
1 tablespoon soy sauce
2 teaspoons rice wine or dry
    sherry
2 teaspoons sugar

Soy Chicken

1 First make the marinade. Put all the ingredients into a shallow dish, stir well to mix, add the chicken and turn to coat. Cover and leave to marinate in the refrigerator for 4 hours or overnight, turning the chicken occasionally.
2 When you are ready to cook, drain the chicken, pouring the marinade into a wok. Place the wok over a moderate heat and stir the marinade until it is bubbling. Add the chicken pieces, stir to mix with the marinade, then simmer very gently, stirring frequently, for 20 minutes or until the chicken is tender. Serve hot.

Serves 3–4
Preparation time: 10 minutes, plus marinating
Cooking time: 25 minutes

1 lb. skinless, boneless chicken
    thighs, cut into 1 inch chunks
MARINADE:
3 tablespoons light soy sauce
3 tablespoons dark soy sauce
2 tablespoons rice wine vinegar or
    white wine or cider vinegar
2 tablespoons brown sugar
2 teaspoons tomato paste
1 garlic clove, crushed
1–2 teaspoons chili powder,
    to taste

Chili Chicken

2 boneless, skinless chicken
   breasts, total weight 8–10 oz.
1 tablespoon peanut oil
1 inch piece of fresh ginger, peeled
   and crushed
1 garlic clove, crushed
1–2 tablespoons chili sauce, to
   taste
1½ cups hot Chicken Stock (see
   page 14)
1 teaspoon cornstarch
1 tablespoon chopped cilantro
salt
MARINADE:
3 tablespoons dark soy sauce
1 tablespoon rice wine
1 teaspoon sugar
TO GARNISH:
½ small red chili, very finely
   chopped
cilantro leaves

This quick-and-easy, spicy hot stir-fry will serve 4 people as part of a Chinese meal, but if you want to serve it simply on its own with rice, there will be enough for 2–3 people.

1 Cut the chicken into thin strips, working diagonally against the grain, and place them in a nonmetallic dish. Mix together the marinade ingredients, pour into the dish and stir to mix. Cover and leave to marinate at room temperature for about 30 minutes.

2 Heat an empty wok until hot. Add the oil and heat until hot. Add the ginger, garlic, and 1 tablespoon chili sauce, stir-fry over a low heat for 1–2 minutes then add the chicken, increase the heat to high and stir-fry for 3 minutes.

3 Pour in about just under 1 cup of the stock and continue stir-frying for 3 minutes or until the chicken is tender.

4 Lift the chicken out of the sauce with a slotted spoon and place it in a warm serving bowl. Add the remaining stock to the wok, stir, then simmer, stirring occasionally, for about 5 minutes. Blend the cornstarch to a paste with a little cold water, pour it into the wok and stir to mix. Simmer, stirring, for 1–2 minutes until the sauce thickens.

5 Stir the cilantro into the sauce, then taste and add salt if necessary, plus more chili sauce if you like. Pour the sauce over the chicken, garnish with chili and cilantro and serve immediately.

Cook's Notes
Bottles of Chinese chili sauce can be found in supermarkets. Brands vary, so take care when using chili sauce for the first time, just in case the one you have chosen is very hot.

Serves 2–4
Preparation time: 5 minutes, plus marinating
Cooking time: about 12 minutes

Kung Pao Chicken

1 egg white
2 teaspoons cornstarch
2 teaspoons soy sauce
2 teaspoons rice wine or dry
   sherry
1 lb. chicken breast fillets, cut into
   bite-sized cubes
2 tablespoons peanut oil
1 large red bell pepper, cored,
   deseeded, and finely chopped
3 dried red chilies, crushed
3 garlic cloves, crushed
2 inch piece of fresh ginger, peeled
   and finely chopped
1 cup shelled unsalted peanuts
SAUCE:
4 teaspoons cornstarch
8 tablespoons Chicken Stock
   (see page 14) or water
2 tablespoons rice wine vinegar or
   white wine or cider vinegar
2 tablespoons soy sauce
1 tablespoon chili sauce
1 tablespoon brown sugar
2 teaspoons tomato paste

This famous dish is said to have been a favourite of a Sichuan governor named Kung Pao.

1 Lightly beat the egg white in a shallow dish with the cornstarch, soy sauce, and rice wine or sherry. Add the cubes of chicken and turn to coat.
2 Prepare the sauce. Blend the cornstarch in a small bowl with 2 tablespoons of the stock or water, then add the remaining stock or water and the remaining ingredients. Stir well to combine.
3 Heat an empty wok until hot. Add the oil and heat until hot. Add the red bell pepper, chilies, garlic, and ginger and stir-fry over a low heat for 2–3 minutes without browning the ingredients.
4 Add about one-quarter of the chicken and marinade, increase the heat to high and stir-fry for 2–3 minutes. Remove with a slotted spoon and set aside. Repeat with the remaining chicken.
5 Pour the sauce mixture into the wok and bring to a boil over a high heat, stirring constantly until thickened and glossy. Return all the chicken to the wok and stir-fry for 2 minutes or until the chicken is tender and evenly coated in the sauce. Stir in the peanuts and serve immediately.

Serves 4
Preparation time: 15 minutes
Cooking time: about 20 minutes

Rapid-fried Chicken Livers with Snow Peas

1 Blend the cornstarch in a small bowl with 2 tablespoons of the stock or water, then add the remaining stock or water, the tomato paste, rice wine or sherry, and lemon juice. Stir well to combine.
2 Heat an empty wok until hot. Add 1 tablespoon of the oil and heat until hot. Add the snow peas and stir-fry over a high heat for 2 minutes. Remove with a slotted spoon and set aside.
3 Heat the remaining oil in the wok over a moderate heat. Add the onion and stir-fry for 2 minutes. Add the chicken livers and garlic and stir-fry for 2–3 minutes until the chicken livers lose their pink color. Pour in the cornstarch mixture and bring it to the boil over a high heat, stirring constantly until thickened and glossy. Lower the heat, add plenty of pepper and simmer gently for 3–5 minutes or until the livers are cooked but still pink in the center.
4 Return the snow peas to the wok, increase the heat to high and toss until hot and evenly combined with the livers. Serve immediately.

Serves 3–4
Preparation time: 10 minutes
Cooking time: about 15 minutes

1 tablespoon cornstarch
8 tablespoons Chicken Stock
   (see page 14) or water
1 tablespoon tomato paste
1 tablespoon rice wine or dry
   sherry
1 teaspoon lemon juice
2 tablespoons peanut oil
½ lb. snow peas, cut in half if large
1 small onion, finely sliced
½ lb. tub frozen chicken livers,
   defrosted, dried and cut into
   1 inch thick slices
1 garlic clove, crushed
pepper

Bonbonji

2 scallions, roughly chopped
2 partially boned chicken breasts,
    with skin on
about 1 cup cold Chicken Stock
    (see page 14)
2–3 inch piece of cucumber
salt and pepper
toasted sesame seeds (see
    page 67), to garnish
DRESSING:
1 tablespoon sesame paste (tahini)
1 tablespoon light soy sauce
2 teaspoons rice wine vinegar or
    white wine or cider vinegar
a few drops of chili oil or 1 teaspoon
    chili sauce, or more to taste
½ teaspoon sugar

This marinated cold chicken salad has a piquant sesame paste dressing. It is garnished with raw cucumber, which provides a cool, crisp, and refreshing contrast to the softness of the chicken.

1 Put the scallions into a wok, then put the chicken breasts skin-side down on top of them, and season with salt and pepper. Cover the chicken with stock and bring to a gentle simmer, then cover the pan with a lid and poach very gently for 15 minutes, turning once.
2 Remove the chicken from the liquid, reserving the liquid, and place it skin-side up on a board. With a rolling pin, pound the chicken to loosen the skin and fibers. Leave it until it is cool enough to handle.
3 Remove and discard the skin and bones from the chicken, then thinly shred the meat. Cut the cucumber into matchsticks, discarding the seeds (and skin if desired). Arrange the pieces of chicken and cucumber in a serving dish.
4 Put all the dressing ingredients into a food processor and add 4 tablespoons of the poaching liquid. Process until all the ingredients are evenly mixed, then taste and add more chili oil or chili sauce if desired. Spoon the dressing over the chicken and cucumber, cover and chill in the refrigerator for about 4 hours.
5 Serve sprinkled with the toasted sesame seeds.

Cook's Notes
If you don't want to go to the trouble of cooking your own chicken, buy ready-cooked chicken from the supermarket and proceed from the beginning of step 3.

Serves 4–6
Preparation time: 30 minutes, plus cooling and chilling
Cooking time: about 20 minutes

Sichuan Chicken with Walnuts

1 egg white
1 tablespoon cornstarch
4 boneless, skinless chicken breasts, each weighing about 5 oz., diced
2 tablespoons peanut oil
½ bunch of scallions, chopped
1 large green bell pepper, cored, deseeded, and diced
2 chilies, deseeded and finely chopped
1 cup walnut pieces
SAUCE:
2 teaspoons cornstarch
4 tablespoons water
2 tablespoons yellow bean sauce
2 tablespoons rice wine or dry sherry
1 teaspoon brown sugar

Ingredients for stir-fries should be of a similar size and shape, so try to cut the chicken, scallions, and green bell pepper into dice the same size as the walnut pieces.

1 First prepare the sauce. Blend the cornstarch to a thin paste with the cold water, then stir in the yellow bean sauce, rice wine or sherry, and sugar.

2 Mix the egg white and cornstarch together in a shallow dish, add the diced chicken and turn to coat.

3 Heat an empty wok until hot. Add the oil and heat until hot. Add the chicken and stir-fry over a high heat for 3–4 minutes or until lightly colored on all sides. Transfer the chicken to a bowl with a slotted spoon.

4 Add the scallions, green bell pepper, and chilies to the wok and stir-fry over a low heat for 2–3 minutes or until softened slightly, taking care not to let the ingredients brown.

5 Stir the sauce to mix, pour it into the wok and increase the heat to high. Return the chicken to the wok and toss for 1–2 minutes or until all the ingredients are combined and piping hot. Add the walnuts and toss for 30 seconds longer. Serve immediately.

Cook's Notes
Take care not to cook the walnuts for longer than 30 seconds otherwise they will discolor the sauce.

Serves 3–4
Preparation time: 15 minutes
Cooking time: about 12 minutes

Strange-flavored Chicken

This oddly-named dish is not strangely flavored at all—it is absolutely delicious. Very hot and spicy, it combines the flavors of sesame, soy, ginger, garlic, and chili. Steamed white rice is the essential accompaniment to act as a foil to the strong flavors.

1 Heat an empty wok until hot. Add the sesame seeds and dry-roast over a low heat until toasted. Tip the sesame seeds out of the wok and set aside.

2 Add the oil to the wok and heat until hot. Add the scallions, ginger, and garlic and stir-fry for 30 seconds. Add the chicken strips, increase the heat to high and stir-fry for 3–4 minutes or until lightly colored on all sides.

3 Add the sesame paste, soy and chili sauces, and the cold water, then toss for 1–2 minutes or until all the ingredients are combined and piping hot. Sprinkle with the sesame oil and toasted sesame seeds and serve immediately.

Cook's Notes

Sesame paste is sold as tahini in supermarkets, health food shops, and Middle Eastern stores.

Serves 3–4
Preparation time: 10 minutes
Cooking time: about 10 minutes

2 tablespoons sesame seeds
2 tablespoons peanut oil
2 tablespoons finely chopped scallions
1 inch piece of fresh ginger, peeled and finely chopped
1 garlic clove, crushed
4 boneless, skinless chicken breasts, each weighing about 5 oz., cut into thin strips against the grain
2 tablespoons sesame paste
2 tablespoons soy sauce
2 tablespoons chili sauce
1 tablespoon water
2 teaspoons sesame oil

Chicken with Pineapple

2 boneless, skinless chicken
    breasts, total weight 8–10 oz.
1 egg white
2 teaspoons cornstarch
⅓–½ cup peanut oil
4 oz. (about 1 cup) pineapple
    chunks, cut into bite-sized
    pieces, with juice reserved
salt and pepper
carrot or orange and spring onion
    julienne strips, to garnish
boiled and drained medium egg
    noodles, to serve
SAUCE:
1 small onion, cut into chunks
1 carrot, cut into julienne strips
1 inch piece of fresh ginger, peeled
    and cut into julienne strips
½ cup cold Chicken Stock (see
    page 14) or water
1 scant cup orange juice
2 tablespoons lemon juice
1 tablespoon light soy sauce
1 tablespoon rice wine vinegar or
    white wine or cider vinegar
1–2 teaspoons sugar, to taste
2 teaspoons cornstarch

Although this dish is very popular in Chinese restaurants in the West, it is often cloyingly sweet. This homemade version is fresh and light, and children love it.

1 Cut the chicken into bite-sized pieces. Put the egg white in a bowl with salt and pepper to taste and whisk with a fork until frothy. Sift in the cornstarch and whisk to mix, then add the chicken and stir until coated.

2 Heat the oil in a wok until very hot but not smoking. Add about one-quarter of the chicken pieces and stir them around so that they separate. Fry for 30–60 seconds until the chicken turns white on all sides. Lift out with a slotted spoon and drain on paper towels. Repeat with the remaining chicken. Very carefully pour off all but about 1 tablespoon of the hot oil from the wok.

3 Return the wok to a low heat and make the sauce. Place the onion, carrot, and ginger in the hot oil and stir-fry for about 3 minutes or until softened, taking care that they do not brown. Pour in the stock or water, orange juice, and lemon juice and increase the heat to high. Bring to a boil, stirring, then add the soy sauce, vinegar, and 1 teaspoon sugar. Stir to mix.

4 Put the chicken into the sauce and cook over a moderate to high heat, stirring occasionally, for 3 minutes. Add the pineapple and juice and cook for 1 further minute.

5 Blend the cornstarch to a paste with a little cold water, then pour it into the wok and stir to mix. Simmer, stirring, for 2 minutes until thickened. Taste for seasoning and add more sugar if liked. Serve hot with boiled and drained egg noodles, sprinkled with carrot or orange and scallion julienne.

Cook's Notes
Cutting a fresh pineapple into chunks is quite tricky, so for this recipe it is a good idea to buy a tub of fresh ripe pineapple chunks—you can get them at most supermarkets. They are packed in their own juice and are perfectly natural, with no additives.

Serves 2–4
Preparation time: 15 minutes
Cooking time: about 20 minutes

Drunken Chicken

8 chicken thighs
1 inch piece of fresh ginger, peeled and thickly sliced
3 scallions, thickly sliced
1 scant cup Shaoxing or Shaohsing rice wine
salt and pepper

1 Put the chicken into a saucepan and sprinkle with the ginger, scallions, and a little salt and pepper. Pour in ¼ cup of the rice wine, then add enough cold water to just cover the chicken.
2 Bring the liquid to a boil over a moderate heat, then turn the heat down to low, cover the pan and simmer for 20 minutes.
3 Turn off the heat under the pan and let the chicken steep in the liquid for 30 minutes. Do not lift the lid during this time.
4 Lift the chicken out of the liquid. If you like, you can remove the skin, although this is not traditional. Put the chicken in a single layer in a nonmetallic dish and pour the remaining rice wine over it. Leave to cool, then cover and chill in the refrigerator for 1–2 days. Turn the chicken over once or twice during this time. Serve cold.

Cook's Notes
In a dish like this, in which the rice wine is the predominant flavor, buy Shaoxing or Shaohsing rice wine from a Chinese supermarket. You will find it tastes far superior to other rice wines, and yet it is not expensive.

Serves 4
Preparation time: 10–15 minutes, plus cooling and chilling
Cooking time: about 25 minutes

Five-Spice Chicken

3 tablespoons peanut oil
4 boneless, skinless chicken breasts, cut into thin strips against the grain
1 onion, thinly sliced
3 carrots, cut into julienne strips
4 oz. cauliflower, divided into tiny florets
1½ teaspoons five-spice powder
½ cup hot Chicken Stock (see page 14) or water
2 tablespoons soy sauce
7 oz. canned water chestnuts, drained and sliced
pepper

1 Heat an empty wok until hot. Add the oil and heat until hot. Add the chicken and stir-fry over a high heat for 3–4 minutes or until lightly colored on all sides. Transfer to a plate with a slotted spoon.
2 Add the onion, carrots, and cauliflower to the wok and sprinkle with the five-spice powder. Stir-fry for 3–4 minutes or until softened, taking care not to let the vegetables brown. Add the stock or water and soy sauce and stir until bubbling.
3 Return the chicken and its juices to the wok and add the water chestnuts. Toss for 1–2 minutes or until all the ingredients are piping hot. Add pepper to taste and serve immediately.

Serves 3–4
Preparation time: 15 minutes
Cooking time: about 15 minutes

White-cut Chicken

"White-cut" is a term used in Chinese cooking to describe chicken or pork that is very gently simmered and steeped in water to produce pale-colored, moist, and tender flesh. The meat is served with a spicy hot sauce, a surprising contrast in both color and flavor.

1 Wash the chicken under cold running water. Put the chicken breast-side up in a large saucepan and cover it generously with cold water (you will need about 4 quarts). Add the slices of ginger and a good pinch of salt, then bring the water to a boil over a moderate heat.

2 Skim off any scum from the surface of the water, then turn the heat down to low and tightly cover the pan. Simmer gently for 30 minutes.

3 Turn off the heat under the pan and let the chicken steep in the liquid for 40 minutes. Do not lift the lid during this time.

4 Remove the chicken from the cooking liquid and immediately plunge it into a large bowl of very cold water (you can add some ice cubes to the water). Leave the chicken in the water for 10–15 minutes, turning it over from time to time, until it is completely cold.

5 Remove the chicken from the water and pat it dry, then put it in a large bowl and cover with plastic wrap. Chill in the refrigerator overnight.

6 To serve, separate the legs and wings from the body of the chicken and chop them crossways into pieces. Chop the chicken breast lengthways in half, then chop each side of the breast crossways into small pieces. Reassemble the bird on a serving platter. Whisk the ingredients for the sauce, then pour it into a small bowl. Serve the chicken as soon as possible, with the bowl of sauce for dipping.

Cook's Notes

For the best flavor, use a fresh free-range chicken.

The chopped chicken is traditionally served as here, reassembled on a large platter. For easier presentation and eating, you may prefer to remove the meat from the bones. You can then slice it thinly and arrange it on individual plates drizzled with the sauce.

Serves 4–6
Preparation time: 20 minutes
Cooking time: about 40 minutes, plus standing, cooling, and chilling

1 chicken, weighing about 3 lb.
1 inch piece of fresh ginger, peeled and thickly sliced
salt
DIPPING SAUCE:
6 tablespoons light or dark soy sauce
1 tablespoon rice wine vinegar or white wine or cider vinegar
2 scallions, sliced into very thin rings
1–2 garlic cloves, very finely chopped, to taste
2 teaspoons sugar
a few cilantro leaves, roughly chopped
½–1 teaspoon chili oil, to taste

Stir-fried Duck with Mango

1 large boneless duck breast
(magret), weighing about
13 oz., or 2 small duck breasts
1 ripe mango
4 tablespoons peanut oil
1 large red chili, sliced into very
thin rings
4 tablespoons rice wine or dry
sherry
3 oz. (1 small bunch) Chinese
mustard greens, shredded
MARINADE:
2 tablespoons light or dark soy
sauce
1 tablespoon rice wine vinegar or
white wine or cider vinegar
½ teaspoon chili oil
1 inch piece of fresh ginger, peeled
and grated
½ teaspoon five-spice powder

In this modern recipe the sweet, juicy fruitiness of mango counteracts the richness of duck meat and tempers the fieriness of red hot chili.

1 Strip the skin and fat off the duck and discard. Cut the duck flesh into thin strips, working diagonally against the grain, then place them in a nonmetallic dish. Mix together the marinade ingredients, pour into the dish and stir to mix. Cover and leave to marinate at room temperature for about 30 minutes.
2 Meanwhile, cut the mango lengthways into three pieces, avoiding the long central stone. Peel the pieces of mango and cut the flesh into strips about the same size as the duck.
3 Heat an empty wok until hot. Add half of the oil and heat until it is hot. Add the duck and stir-fry over a high heat for 4–5 minutes or until just tender. Remove the duck with a slotted spoon and repeat with the remaining oil and duck.
4 Return all of the duck to the wok and sprinkle with the chili and rice wine or sherry. Toss to mix, then add the mango and mustard greens and toss for 1–2 minutes, just until the greens start to wilt. Serve immediately.

Cook's Notes
Chinese mustard greens are also called gai choy. You can buy them in Asian specialty stores, farmers' markets, and in some supermarkets. As their name suggests, they have a pungent, mustard flavor. If you can't get them, use peppery rocket or watercress. For a milder flavor, use spinach.

Serves 2–4
Preparation time: 15 minutes, plus marinating
Cooking time: 10–15 minutes

'Study the past, if you would divine the future.'

Confucius

Aromatic Crispy Duck

1 large boneless duck breast
   (magret), weighing about
   13 oz., or 2 small duck breasts
2 tablespoons rice wine or dry
   sherry
1 teaspoon salt
¼ teaspoon five-spice powder
TO SERVE:
hoisin sauce
plum sauce

Peking Duck is a classic, restaurant-style dish that is time-consuming and difficult to achieve at home. This modern recipe is a play on the theme but using duck breasts. Although it is not the same thing as Peking Duck, it is quicker, easier, and infinitely more practical, and the end result is very good.

1 If you are using 1 large duck breast, cut it diagonally in half. Score diagonal lines in the skin of the duck breasts, cutting through the fat just to the meat below. Place the duck in a dish and pour 1 tablespoon rice wine or sherry over each breast, then rub with the salt. Leave the dish, uncovered, at cool room temperature for at least 4 hours, or overnight if possible.

2 Heat an empty wok until hot. Place the duck breasts, skin-side down, in the wok and cook over a moderate to high heat for 5 minutes until the skin is browned and crisp. While the duck is cooking, press it down hard with a spatula to keep the breasts as flat as possible.

3 Transfer the duck breasts, skin-side up, to a rack in a roasting tin. Drizzle or brush a little of the hot fat from the wok over the skin and sprinkle with the five-spice powder. Roast in a preheated oven at 425°F for 5 minutes for rare duck, 10 minutes for medium.

4 Transfer the duck to a carving board and slice it very thinly, following the diagonal lines in the skin. Arrange on warmed plates with pools of hoisin and plum sauces. Serve hot.

Cook's Notes
If you like, serve the duck Peking style with pancakes and shredded scallions. In step 4, cut the crispy skin off the top of the breasts and slice it into very thin strips, then cut the duck meat into thin strips as well.

Serves 2
Preparation time: 10 minutes, plus standing
Cooking time: 10–15 minutes
Oven temperature: 425°F

Quick-fried Ribbons of Duck with Plum & Ginger Sauce

1 Heat an empty wok until hot. Add the oil and heat until hot. Add the strips of duck and stir-fry over a high heat for 4–5 minutes. Remove the duck with a slotted spoon and set aside.

2 Add the plums to the wok with the stock or water, hoisin sauce, orange juice, sugar, soy sauce, ginger, and five-spice powder. Stir-fry to mix, then lower the heat and simmer for about 10 minutes or until the plums are soft.

3 Return the duckling to the wok, increase the heat to high and boil rapidly until the duckling is tender and glazed with the sauce. Serve immediately, garnished with scallion slices.

Serves 2–3
Preparation time: 15 minutes
Cooking time: about 20 minutes

I tablespoon peanut oil
I large boneless duck breast
    (magret), weighing about
    13 oz., or 2 small duck breasts,
    skin and fat removed, cut into
    thin strips
½ lb. red plums, halved, stoned and
    cut into thin strips
4 tablespoons hot Chicken Stock
    (see page 14) or water
I tablespoon hoisin sauce
2 teaspoons orange juice
2 teaspoons granulated sugar
I teaspoon soy sauce
½ teaspoon ground ginger
¼ teaspoon five-spice powder
scallion slices, to garnish

beef, lamb, & pork

When the Chinese cook beef, lamb, or pork, the emphasis is on freshness, tenderness, and flavor. This is guaranteed when exquisitely cut slices of meat are rapidly stir-fried and married with a dazzling partnership of ingredients—beef with tangerine, say, or paper-thin lamb with garlic, or pork glazed with honey. Lamb was introduced to the north of China during the Mongol and Tartar invasions; cattle and pigs were indigenous, and part of Chinese legend.

Tangerine Beef

1 piece of rump steak, weighing
　　about 12 oz., trimmed of all fat
3 tablespoons peanut oil
4 shallots, cut lengthways into
　　chunks
1 scant cup beef stock or water
2 tablespoons soy sauce
2 tablespoons rice wine or dry
　　sherry
3 tangerines, peeled and
　　segmented, with their juice
1 green chili, deseeded and very
　　finely chopped
1–2 teaspoons sugar, to taste
salt and pepper
1 small handful of cilantro leaves,
　　roughly chopped, to finish
MARINADE:
2 pieces of dried citrus fruit peel
2 tablespoons soy sauce
1 tablespoon rice wine vinegar or
　　white wine or cider vinegar
1 tablespoon cornstarch
1 teaspoon sugar

Beef is often teamed with citrus fruit and citrus peel in northern Chinese stir-fries. This recipe is a modern adaptation of this classic combination, using sweet and dainty tangerines. Bright and colorful, it is the perfect dish for winter when tangerines are in season.

1 Wrap the beef in plastic wrap and place it in the freezer for 1–2 hours until it is just hard. Meanwhile, soak the pieces of citrus peel for the marinade in hot water for about 30 minutes until softened, then drain and chop finely.

2 Remove the beef from the freezer and unwrap it, then slice it into thin strips, working against the grain. Put the strips in a nonmetallic dish. Whisk together all the marinade ingredients, pour the marinade over the beef and stir to mix. Leave to marinate at room temperature for about 30 minutes or until the beef is completely thawed out.

3 Heat an empty wok until hot. Add 1 tablespoon of the oil and heat until hot. Add about half of the beef and stir-fry over a high heat for 3 minutes. Transfer to a plate with a slotted spoon and repeat with another tablespoon of the oil and the remaining beef.

4 Heat the remaining oil in the wok, then add the shallots, stock or water, soy sauce, rice wine, or sherry and the juice from the tangerines. Sprinkle in the chili, sugar, and a little salt and pepper. Bring to the boil, stirring, then stir-fry for about 5 minutes until the liquid has reduced.

5 Return the beef to the wok and toss vigorously for 1–2 minutes until all the ingredients are combined and coated with sauce. Add about two-thirds of the tangerine segments and toss quickly to mix, then taste for seasoning. Serve hot, strewn with the remaining tangerine segments and the cilantro.

Cook's Notes
Dried citrus fruit peel is sold in packets in Chinese supermarkets. It has a sharp, bittersweet tang, which is delicious in stir-fries.

　　Take care to remove the membranes from the tangerines when segmenting them. Peel the whole fruit, then slice vertically between the membranes to release the segments. Hold the fruit over a bowl to catch the juice and squeeze the membranes at the finish to extract any remaining juice.

Serves 2–3
Preparation time: about 15 minutes, plus freezing and marinating
Cooking time: 15 minutes

Beef with Shiitake Mushrooms & Ginger

4 oz. dried shiitake mushrooms
³/₄ cup hot water
2 tablespoons peanut oil
I garlic clove, crushed
¼ lb. rump steak, trimmed of all fat
   and sliced into thin strips
   against the grain
2 tablespoons finely chopped fresh
   ginger
I tablespoon black bean sauce
¼ teaspoon pepper
I teaspoon sugar
4 scallions, chopped
½ cup hot Chicken Stock (see page
   14)
2 scallions, shredded, to garnish

1 Soak the mushrooms in the hot water for 30 minutes. Drain and squeeze out excess liquid, slice the caps and discard any hard stalks.
2 Heat an empty wok until hot. Add the oil and heat until hot. Add the garlic and stir-fry over a low heat for 30–60 seconds until golden. Add the beef, ginger, black bean sauce, pepper, and sugar. Increase the heat to high and stir-fry for a few minutes until the beef is lightly browned. Stir in the mushrooms, scallions, and stock and stir-fry for 5 minutes. Serve immediately, garnished with shredded scallion.

Serves 2–3
Preparation time: 10 minutes, plus soaking
Cooking time: 10 minutes

Beef with Bok Choy in Oyster Sauce

This is a classic dish from the Cantonese region of China. Bok choy, sometimes also called bok choi or pak choi, is excellent in stir-fries. It has a crisp texture, is juicy when bitten into, and has a mild mustard flavor. Take care not to overcook it or you will lose its best qualities. If you are unable to obtain it, use rocket, spinach, or Swiss chard instead.

1 First make the marinade. Put the garlic into a shallow dish with the soy sauce, rice wine or sherry, and sugar. Add the beef strips and turn to coat. Leave to marinate for about 30 minutes, turning the meat occasionally.

2 Heat an empty wok until hot. Add 2 tablespoons of the oil and heat until hot. Add the beef and its marinade and stir-fry over a high heat for 3–4 minutes or until browned on all sides. Remove the wok from the heat and tip the beef and its juices into a bowl.

3 Return the wok to a moderate heat. Add the remaining oil and heat until hot. Add the bok choy, scallions, ginger, and salt and stir-fry for 1–2 minutes or until the bok-choy is just starting to wilt.

4 Return the beef and its juices to the wok, add the oyster sauce and increase the heat to high. Toss until all the ingredients are evenly combined. Add pepper to taste and serve immediately, with deep-fried seaweed, if desired.

Serves 3–4
Preparation time: 15 minutes, plus marinating
Cooking time: about 10 minutes

1 lb. rump steak, trimmed of all fat and sliced into thin strips against the grain
3 tablespoons peanut oil
10 oz. bok choy, shredded
5 scallions, thinly sliced on the diagonal
1 inch piece of fresh ginger, peeled and finely chopped
½ teaspoon salt
2 tablespoons oyster sauce
pepper
deep-fried seaweed (optional)
MARINADE:
2 garlic cloves, crushed
3 tablespoons soy sauce
2 tablespoons rice wine or dry sherry
1 teaspoon sugar

'Learning is a treasure which accompanies its owner everywhere.'

Chinese Proverb

Sizzling Beef

1 piece of rump steak, weighing
    about 12 oz., trimmed of all fat
2 inch piece of fresh ginger, peeled
    and grated
2 garlic cloves, crushed
1 tablespoon cornstarch
2 teaspoons sugar
about ¾ cup peanut oil, for frying
2 carrots cut into matchsticks
3 celery sticks cut into matchsticks
¾ cup hot beef stock or water
1 tablespoon soy sauce
1–2 tablespoons chili sauce, to
    taste
salt and pepper

You can make this very tasty stir-fry from everyday ingredients that are easy to find in any supermarket. It looks and tastes good served with egg noodles, which only take a few minutes to cook.

1 Wrap the beef in plastic wrap and place it in the freezer for 1–2 hours until it is just hard.

2 Remove the beef from the freezer and unwrap it, then slice it into very thin shreds, working against the grain. Place the shreds in a nonmetallic dish, add the ginger, garlic, cornstarch, and half of the sugar and stir to mix. Leave to marinate at room temperature for about 30 minutes or until the beef is completely thawed out.

3 Heat the oil in a wok until very hot but not smoking. Add a small batch of beef strips and fry for 1–2 minutes or until the meat is browned on all sides. Stir the strips constantly during frying so they keep separate. Lift out with a slotted spoon and drain on paper towels. Repeat with the remaining beef.

4 Very carefully pour off all but about 1 tablespoon of the hot oil from the wok. Add the carrots and stir-fry over a high heat for 2 minutes, then add the celery and pour in the stock or water. Toss and stir-fry for about 4 minutes until the liquid has been absorbed by the vegetables.

5 Add the soy sauce and 1 tablespoon of the chili sauce, then return all of the beef to the wok and sprinkle with the remaining sugar and salt and pepper to taste. Toss vigorously over the highest possible heat for 1–2 minutes until all the ingredients are shiny and sizzling. Taste and add more chili sauce if liked. Serve very hot.

Cook's Notes
Keep fresh ginger in the freezer. Frozen ginger is much easier to peel and grate than fresh.

Serves 2–3
Preparation time: about 15 minutes, plus freezing and marinating
Cooking time: about 20 minutes

Ma Po's Minced Beef

2 teaspoons cornstarch
½ cup cold water
2 tablespoons soy sauce
2 tablespoons hoisin sauce
2 teaspoons chili sauce
1 teaspoon dark brown sugar
2 tablespoons peanut oil
¼ lb. minced beef
2 teaspoons black bean sauce
6 button mushrooms, peeled and
    quartered lengthways
4 scallions, sliced into thin rings
3 garlic cloves, crushed
10 oz. bean curd (tofu), drained,
    dried and diced
1 tablespoon sesame oil
TO SERVE:
½–2 teaspoons chili oil, to taste
rice noodles, (optional)

Bean curd (tofu) is a highly nutritious food, often used in oriental cooking as a form of inexpensive protein. In this recipe it makes a little meat go a long way.

1 Blend the cornstarch in a small bowl with ¼ cup of the cold water, then add the remaining cold water, the soy, hoisin and chili sauces, and the sugar. Stir well to combine.
2 Heat an empty wok until hot. Add the oil and heat until hot. Add the meat and black bean sauce, the mushrooms, and half of the scallions. Stir-fry over a high heat for 3–4 minutes. Add the garlic, the cornstarch mixture, and bean curd and bring to a boil, stirring until thickened and glossy. Stir-fry for a further 2 minutes, then sprinkle with the remaining scallions and the sesame oil. Serve drizzled with chili oil to taste, accompanied by rice noodles if desired.

Serves 2–4
Preparation time: 10 minutes
Cooking time: about 10 minutes

'One cannot manage too many affairs: like pumpkins in the water, one pops up while you try to hold down the other.'

Chinese Proverb

Chili Beef

2 tablespoons peanut oil
1 bunch of scallions, roughly
   chopped
12 oz. minced beef
1 cup beef stock made from cube
2 tablespoons black bean sauce
2 tablespoons chili sauce, or to
   taste
1 teaspoon dark brown sugar
10 oz. silken bean curd (tofu),
   drained and diced
salt

Bottled chili sauce can be found in most large supermarkets as well as oriental stores. The amount you use depends on the brand—some are far hotter than others—and your own personal taste of course. Silken bean curd (tofu) is also sold at supermarkets and oriental stores, as well as at health food shops; it is not essential for this dish, but it is more suitable than ordinary tofu as it is less firm and will blend better with the minced beef.

1 Heat an empty wok until hot. Add the oil and heat until hot. Add half of the scallions and stir-fry over a low heat for 1–2 minutes or until slightly softened. Add the beef, increase the heat to high, and stir-fry for 3–4 minutes or until browned on all sides, pressing well to remove any lumps in the meat.

2 Add the stock, black bean and chili sauces, and sugar and bring to the boil, stirring. Lower the heat, cover the wok with a lid and cook for 10–15 minutes or until the beef mixture is reduced and thickened, stirring frequently.

3 Add the bean curd and stir in gently. Heat through, then taste and add salt if necessary, plus more chili sauce if desired. Serve immediately, sprinkled with the remaining chopped scallions.

Serves 4
Preparation time: 10 minutes
Cooking time: about 25 minutes

'To be able to praise five things everywhere under heaven constitutes perfect virtue...gravity, generosity of soul, sincerity, earnestness, and kindness.'

Confucius

Stir-fried Beef with Baby Corn & Red Pepper

1 Heat an empty wok until hot. Add the Sichuan peppercorns and dry-roast over a low heat for 1–2 minutes. Remove from the wok and crush using a mortar and pestle.

2 Prepare the sauce. Put all the ingredients into a bowl or jar and stir well to mix.

3 Heat an empty wok until hot. Add 2 tablespoons of the oil and heat until hot. Add the beef strips, chilies, and crushed peppercorns and stir-fry over a high heat for 3–4 minutes or until the beef is browned on all sides. Remove the wok from the heat and tip the beef and its juices into a bowl.

4 Return the wok to a moderate heat, add the remaining oil and heat until hot. Add the onion, red bell pepper and stir-fry for 2–3 minutes or until slightly softened, then add the baby corn and stir-fry for 1–2 minutes or until hot.

5 Return the beef and its juices to the wok, pour in the sauce, and increase the heat to high. Toss for 2–3 minutes or until all the ingredients are combined and piping hot. Serve immediately.

Serves 3–4
Preparation time: 10–15 minutes
Cooking time: about 15 minutes

1 tablespoon Sichuan peppercorns
3 tablespoons peanut oil
1 lb. rump steak, trimmed of all fat and cut into thin strips against the grain
2 green chilies, deseeded and finely chopped
1 onion, finely sliced
1 red bell pepper, cored, deseeded, and cut lengthways into thin strips
14 oz. baby corn
SAUCE:
3 tablespoons soy sauce
2 tablespoons rice wine or dry sherry
1 tablespoon dark brown sugar
1 teaspoon five-spice powder

Beef with Broccoli & Oyster Sauce

1 piece of rump steak, weighing
    about 12 oz., trimmed of all fat
1 egg white
2 tablespoons soy sauce
2 garlic cloves, crushed
1 inch piece of fresh ginger, peeled
    and grated
1 tablespoon cornstarch
1 teaspoon sugar
about ¾ cup peanut oil, for frying
½ lb. broccoli, divided into small
    florets
½ cup rice wine or dry sherry
3 tablespoons oyster sauce
2 tablespoons soy sauce, or more
    to taste
salt and pepper
TO FINISH:
sesame oil
2 tablespoons toasted
    sesame seeds

Beef in oyster sauce is a classic and popular pairing in Cantonese cookery. The oyster doesn't flavor the meat with fish, but gives it a special rich and tasty savoriness.

1 Wrap the beef in plastic wrap and place it in the freezer for 1–2 hours until it is just hard.

2 Remove the beef from the freezer and unwrap it, then slice it into rectangles about the size of a large postage stamp, working against the grain. Whisk the egg white in a nonmetallic dish, add the soy sauce, garlic, ginger, cornstarch, and sugar and whisk to mix. Add the beef, stir to coat, then leave to marinate at room temperature for about 30 minutes or until the beef is completely thawed out.

3 Heat the oil in a wok until very hot but not smoking. Add about one-third of the beef rectangles and stir them around so they separate. Fry for 30–60 seconds until the beef changes color on all sides, lift out with a slotted spoon, and drain on paper towels. Repeat with the remaining beef. Very carefully pour off all but about 2 tablespoons of the hot oil from the wok.

4 Add the broccoli florets to the wok, sprinkle with the rice wine or sherry, and toss over a moderate heat for 3 minutes. Return the beef to the wok and add the oyster sauce and soy sauce. Increase the heat to high and stir-fry vigorously for 3–4 minutes or until the beef and broccoli are tender. Taste for seasoning, and add more soy sauce if desired. Serve hot, drizzled with a little sesame oil, and sprinkled with toasted sesame seeds.

Serves 2–3
Preparation time: about 15 minutes, plus freezing, and marinating
Cooking time: 15–20 minutes

Yellow Flower Lamb

12 oz. lamb neck fillet
2 eggs
4 scallions, finely chopped
2½ tablespoons peanut oil
½ oz. dried shiitake mushrooms
1 inch piece of fresh ginger, peeled
    and finely chopped
3 oz. canned sliced bamboo
    shoots, drained
2 tablespoons soy sauce
2 tablespoons rice wine or dry
    sherry
1 teaspoon dark brown sugar
½ teaspoon five-spice powder
salt and pepper
1 tablespoon sesame oil, to finish

The pretty omelette garnish on top of this simple stir-fry gives it its name.

1 Wrap the lamb in plastic wrap and place it in the freezer for
1–2 hours until it is just hard.
2 Meanwhile, beat the eggs in a bowl with half of the scallions and
salt and pepper to taste. Heat an empty wok until hot. Add
2 teaspoons of the oil and heat until hot. Add the egg mixture and
tilt the wok to make a flat omelette. Slide the omelette out of the
pan on to a plate or board and roll up tightly; set aside.
3 Cook the dried mushrooms in boiling water for 10 minutes.
Drain and slice thinly. Cut the lamb into thin strips against the grain,
discarding any fat and sinew. Leave it at room temperature for about
30 minutes or until the meat is completely thawed out
4 Heat the empty wok until hot. Add the remaining oil and heat
until hot. Add the remaining scallions and the ginger and stir-fry
over a low heat for a few seconds to flavor the oil. Add the lamb,
increase the heat to high and stir-fry for 2–3 minutes until browned
on all sides. Add the mushrooms, bamboo shoots, soy sauce, rice
wine or sherry, sugar, and five-spice powder. Stir-fry for 1–2 minutes
or until the lamb is tender and all the ingredients are hot and evenly
combined.
5 Transfer the lamb to a warmed serving dish. Slice the rolled
omelette into thin rings, then arrange them on top of the lamb to
resemble flower petals. Sprinkle with the sesame oil and serve
immediately.

Serves 3–4
Preparation time: 15 minutes, plus freezing
Cooking time: about 25 minutes

Quick-fried Lamb with Leeks

1 Wrap the lamb in plastic wrap and place it in the freezer for 1–2 hours until it is just hard. Cut it into thin strips against the grain, discarding any fat and sinew. Leave at room temperature for about 30 minutes or until the meat is completely thawed out.

2 Heat an empty wok until hot. Add the oil and heat until hot. Add the meat and stir-fry over a high heat for 2–3 minutes until browned on all sides. Add the leeks, ginger, and garlic and stir-fry for 1 minute, then add the soy sauce, vinegar, sugar, salt, and half of the five-spice powder. Stir-fry for 30–60 seconds or until the meat is tender and all the ingredients are evenly combined. Serve immediately, sprinkled with the remaining five-spice powder.

Serves 4

Preparation time: 15 minutes, plus freezing
Cooking time: about 10 minutes

12 oz. slice of leg of lamb
3 tablespoons peanut oil
4 leeks, diagonally cut into 1½ inch lengths, washed, drained ,and dried
1 inch piece of fresh ginger, peeled and finely chopped
2 garlic cloves, crushed
2 tablespoons soy sauce
2 teaspoons rice wine vinegar or white wine or cider vinegar
½ teaspoon dark brown sugar
¼ teaspoon salt
1 teaspoon five-spice powder

'Although there exist many different subjects for elegant conversation, there are persons who cannot meet a cripple without talking about feet.'

Chinese Proverb

Lamb with Spicy Hot Sauce

1 lb. lamb neck fillet
3 tablespoons peanut oil
4 scallions, thinly sliced on the
    diagonal
2 garlic cloves, crushed
6–8 small fresh chilies, to garnish
    (optional)
bean thread noodles, to serve
SAUCE:
2 teaspoons cornstarch
4 tablespoons cold water
2 tablespoons hot chili sauce
1 tablespoon rice wine vinegar or
    white wine or cider vinegar
2 teaspoons dark brown sugar
½ teaspoon five-spice powder

Take care. This simple stir-fry is fiery hot.

1 Wrap the lamb in plastic wrap and place it in the freezer for 1–2 hours until it is just hard. Cut it into thin strips against the grain, discarding any fat and sinew. Leave at room temperature for about 30 minutes or until the meat is completely thawed out.
2 Prepare the sauce. Blend the cornstarch to a thin paste with the cold water, then stir in the chili sauce, vinegar, sugar, and five-spice powder.
3 Heat an empty wok until hot. Add 2 tablespoons of the oil and heat until hot. Add the lamb and stir-fry over a high heat for 3–4 minutes or until browned on all sides. Remove the wok from the heat and tip the lamb and its juices into a bowl.
4 Return the wok to a moderate heat. Add the remaining oil and heat until hot. Add the scallions and garlic and stir-fry for 30 seconds. Remove with a slotted spoon.
5 Stir the sauce to mix, pour it into the wok, and increase the heat to high. Stir until the sauce thickens, then add the lamb and its juices and the scallion mixture. Toss for 1–2 minutes or until piping hot. Serve immediately, with bean thread noodles. Garnish with a few small chilies if desired.

Serves 3–4
Preparation time: 10 minutes, plus freezing
Cooking time: about 10 minutes

Sichuan Kidneys

8 lambs' kidneys
½ teaspoon baking soda
1 teaspoon rice wine vinegar or
   white wine or cider vinegar
½ teaspoon salt
1 teaspoon Sichuan peppercorns
2 tablespoons peanut oil
1 inch piece of fresh ginger, peeled
   and finely chopped
4 scallions, finely chopped
2 garlic cloves, finely chopped
½ teaspoon hot chili powder, or
   more to taste
SAUCE:
2 teaspoons cornstarch
4 tablespoons cold water
2 tablespoons soy sauce
2 tablespoons rice wine or dry
   sherry
½ teaspoon brown sugar

1 Remove any membrane from around the kidneys, then cut each kidney in half lengthways. Cut out and discard the cores from the centers and discard any fat. With a sharp knife, score the outer surface of each kidney half in a criss-cross pattern, then cut the kidneys into small pieces. Place the kidneys in a bowl, sprinkle over the baking soda, and turn to coat. Leave to stand for about 20 minutes.

2 Rinse the kidneys under cold running water, then return them to the bowl and add the vinegar and salt. Turn to coat, then transfer them to a sieve and leave them to drain for about 30 minutes.

3 Meanwhile, prepare the sauce. Blend the cornstarch to a thin paste with the cold water, then stir in the soy sauce, rice wine or sherry, and sugar. Set aside.

4 Heat an empty wok until hot. Add the Sichuan peppercorns and dry-fry over a low heat for 1–2 minutes. Remove from the wok and crush using a mortar and pestle.

5 Pat the kidneys dry with paper towels. Add the oil to the wok and heat until hot. Add the kidneys and stir-fry over a moderate heat for about 1 minute, then add the ginger, scallions, garlic, crushed peppercorns, and chili powder and stir-fry for 2–3 minutes.

6 Stir the sauce to mix, pour it into the wok and stir for 1–2 minutes or until bubbling. Serve immediately.

Serves 2–3
Preparation time: 20 minutes, plus standing and draining
Cooking time: about 10 minutes

'When you meet someone better than yourself, turn your thoughts to becoming his equal. When you meet someone not as good as yourself, look within and examine your own self.'

Confucius

Paper-thin Lamb with Garlic and Spring Onions

1 Wrap the lamb in plastic wrap and place it in the freezer for 1–2 hours until it is just hard. Cut it into paper-thin slices against the grain, discarding any fat and sinew. Leave at room temperature for about 30 minutes or until completely thawed out.

2 Heat an empty wok until hot. Add the peanut oil and heat until hot. Add the garlic and stir-fry over a low heat for a few seconds to flavor the oil, then add the lamb and sprinkle with the chili powder, sugar, and salt. Increase the heat to high and stir-fry for 3–4 minutes until the lamb is browned on all sides.

3 Add the scallions, soy sauce, and rice wine or sherry and stir-fry for 30–60 seconds or until all the ingredients are quite dry. Serve immediately, sprinkled with the sesame oil.

Serves 3–4

Preparation time: 10 minutes, plus freezing
Cooking time: about 6 minutes

1 lb. lamb neck fillet
2 tablespoons peanut oil
3 large garlic cloves, thinly sliced
½ teaspoon chili powder, or to taste
½ teaspoon dark brown sugar
pinch of salt
1 large bunch of scallions, cut into 3 inch lengths and shredded lengthways
2 tablespoons soy sauce
2 tablespoons rice wine or dry sherry
2 teaspoons sesame oil

Red-cooked Pork

2 lb. boned, rolled, and tied pork
   shoulder joint
I teaspoon five-spice powder
I tablespoon peanut oil
I quart cold Chicken Stock (see
   page 14) or water
I cup dark soy sauce
2 inch piece of fresh ginger, peeled
   and thinly sliced
2 pieces of star anise
2 teaspoons sugar
salt and pepper
GRAVY:
I small fresh red chili, sliced into
   rings
I teaspoon tomato paste
I teaspoon cornstarch

The term "red-cooked" refers to food that is braised in soy sauce. White meats like chicken and pork are most often used for red-cooking. This recipe is a Western-style adaptation of the classic Chinese cooking technique—the pork is sliced after braising and served with a gravy made from the cooking juices. It makes an excellent Sunday lunch, served with stir-fried vegetables.

1 Rub the pork all over with the five-spice powder, a little salt, and plenty of pepper. Heat the oil in a flameproof casserole, add the pork and cook over a moderate heat until browned on all sides.

2 Pour in the stock or water, then add the soy sauce, ginger, star anise, and sugar and bring to a boil. Lower the heat, cover the casserole, and simmer very gently for 1½ hours or until the pork is tender when pierced with a skewer. Turn the joint over twice during the cooking time.

3 Remove the pork from the liquid and set aside, covered with foil, for 10–15 minutes. Meanwhile, make the gravy. Strain 1 cup of the cooking liquid into a saucepan, add the chili and tomato paste and bring to the boil. Blend the cornstarch to a paste with a little cold water, pour into the sauce, and stir to mix. Simmer, stirring, for 1–2 minutes until the sauce thickens, then taste and adjust the seasoning.

4 Carve the pork into slices, discarding the string and rind, then arrange the slices on warmed dinner plates. Spoon the gravy around the pork and serve immediately.

Serves 4–6
Preparation time: 15 minutes
Cooking time: 1 hour 40 minutes

Crispy Pork with Orange & Vegetables

4 oz. baby corn
4 oz. baby carrots
4 oz. green beans, halved if large
1 egg white
1 tablespoon cornstarch
1 lb. pork fillet (tenderloin), cut
   into thin strips against the grain
about ¾ cup peanut oil, for frying
4 scallions, thinly sliced on the
   diagonal
1 inch piece of fresh ginger, finely
   chopped
1–2 garlic cloves, crushed
salt and pepper
SAUCE:
2 teaspoons cornstarch
6 tablespoons Chicken Stock
   (see page 14) or water
finely grated rind and juice of
   1 large orange
2 tablespoons soy sauce
¼ teaspoon five-spice powder

1 Boil the baby corn and carrots in separate pans of salted water for 3 minutes. Boil the green beans for 2 minutes in the same way.
2 Prepare the sauce. Blend the cornstarch with 2 tablespoons of the stock or water, then add the remaining stock or water, the orange rind and juice, soy sauce, and five-spice powder. Stir well.
3 Beat the egg white, cornstarch, and a pinch of salt. Add the pork and turn to coat. Heat the oil in a wok until hot but not smoking. Pan-fry the pork in batches for 2–3 minutes or until crispy. Lift out with a slotted spoon, drain on paper towels, and keep hot.
4 Carefully pour off all but 1–2 tablespoons of oil from the wok. Add the scallions, ginger, and garlic and stir-fry over a low heat for 2–3 minutes without browning. Add the vegetables, increase the heat to high, and stir-fry until heated through. Add the cornstarch mixture and boil over a high heat, stirring constantly until thick and glossy. Add salt and pepper to taste. Serve immediately, with the crispy pork.

Serves 4
Preparation time: 15–20 minutes
Cooking time: 20 minutes

Barbecued Pork

2 lb. pork shoulder
shredded scallions, to garnish
MARINADE:
2 tablespoons soy sauce
2 tablespoons rice wine or dry
   sherry
2 teaspoons sesame oil
1 teaspoon salt
2 teaspoons ginger juice (squeezed
   from chopped fresh root
   ginger)
2 tablespoons honey
¼ cup sugar
2 garlic cloves, crushed

1 Trim any excess fat from the pork and cut the meat into 2 x 2 x 4 inch slices. Mix together all the ingredients for the marinade in a dish.
2 Add the pork to the marinade, cover, and leave to marinate for at least 6 hours in the refrigerator. Turn the meat occasionally so that it is well coated with the marinade.
3 Place the pork on a wire rack in a roasting pan. Roast in a preheated oven at 350°F for 40–45 minutes, or until tender. Baste the pork frequently with the pan juices.
4 Cut the cooked pork into serving pieces and arrange them on a plate. Garnish with scallions and serve immediately.

Serves 4–6
Preparation time: 10 minutes, plus marinating
Cooking time: 40–45 minutes

Stir-fried Pork with Bean Curd & Snow Peas

1 First prepare the sauce. Blend the cornstarch to a paste with 2 tablespoons of the stock or water, then stir in the remaining stock or water and the remaining ingredients.

2 Heat an empty wok until hot. Add 2 tablespoons of the peanut oil and heat until hot. Add the pork strips and stir-fry over a high heat for 3–4 minutes or until lightly colored on all sides. Remove the wok from the heat and tip the pork and its juices into a bowl.

3 Return the wok to a moderate heat. Add the remaining peanut oil and heat until hot. Add the bean curd and stir-fry for 1–2 minutes or until lightly colored on all sides. Remove the wok from the heat and transfer the bean curd to paper towels with a slotted spoon. Keep hot.

4 Return the wok to the heat and add the snow peas and garlic. Stir-fry for 2 minutes. Return the pork and its juices to the wok, add the Chinese cabbage and stir-fry for 30 seconds, just until mixed with the pork and snow peas.

5 Stir the sauce to mix, then pour it into the wok. Increase the heat to high and stir for 1–2 minutes or until the sauce thickens. Gently fold in the bean curd. Add pepper to taste and sprinkle with the sesame oil. Serve immediately.

Serves 3–4
Preparation time: 15–20 minutes
Cooking time: about 15 minutes

3 tablespoons peanut oil
12 oz. pork fillet (tenderloin), cut
   into thin strips against the grain
8–10 oz. firm bean curd (tofu),
   drained, dried and cut into
   cubes
4 oz. snow peas, trimmed
2 garlic cloves, crushed
8 oz. Chinese cabbage, shredded
pepper
1 teaspoon sesame oil, to finish
SAUCE:
2 teaspoons cornstarch
6 tablespoons Chicken Stock
   (see page 14) or water
3 tablespoons soy sauce
2 tablespoons rice wine or dry
   sherry
½ teaspoon five-spice powder
½ teaspoon chili powder, or
   to taste

'Fine words and an insinuating appearance are seldom associated with true virtue.'

Confucius

Sweet & Spicy Pork with Pomegranate

1 pork fillet (tenderloin), weighing
   about 12 oz.
4 tablespoons peanut oil
4–6 scallions, roughly chopped
1 inch piece of fresh ginger, peeled
   and finely chopped
2 garlic cloves, finely chopped
2–3 carrots, very thinly sliced on
   the diagonal
4 oz. bean sprouts
seeds of 1 pomegranate
salt and pepper
SAUCE:
4 tablespoons rice wine or dry
   sherry
2 tablespoons soy sauce, or more
   to taste
2 tablespoons chili sauce, or more
   to taste
2 tablespoons honey
1 tablespoon tomato paste
2 teaspoons cornstarch

Pomegranate seeds and bean sprouts add crunch to the tender nuggets of pork in this modern stir-fry.

1 Cut the pork fillet crossways into ¾ inch slices, then cut these slices crossways into 2–3 strips. Mix the sauce ingredients in a 2-cup measuring cup, add cold water up to the 1 cup mark and stir well to mix.

2 Heat an empty wok until hot. Add the oil and heat until very hot. Add the scallions, ginger, and garlic and stir-fry over a moderate heat for 1 minute. Add the carrots and stir-fry for 1–2 minutes.

3 Increase the heat to high, add the pork and stir-fry for 5 minutes. Pour in the sauce mixture and bring to the boil, stirring all the time, then simmer for about 2 minutes or until the sauce is thick and reduced. Taste for seasoning and add more soy sauce or chili sauce if desired.

4 Add the bean sprouts and toss vigorously to mix all the ingredients together. Sprinkle with the pomegranate seeds and serve immediately.

Cook's Notes
To extract the seeds from a pomegranate, cut the fruit in half, then pick out the seeds with a toothpick or skewer. Work over a mixing bowl, as the juice stains.

Serves 2–4
Preparation time: 30 minutes
Cooking time: about 15 minutes

Hot & Sour Pork

12 oz. pork fillet (tenderloin), cut into ¼ inch thick slices against the grain
3 tablespoons soy sauce
2 tablespoons rice wine vinegar or white wine or cider vinegar
2 teaspoons cornstarch
1 inch piece of fresh ginger, peeled
1 large garlic clove
2 dried red chilies, roughly chopped
4 tablespoons peanut oil
1 large red bell pepper, cored, deseeded, and cut lengthways into thin strips
8 oz. snow peas, trimmed
10 oz. firm bean curd (tofu), drained, dried and sliced
½ cup Chicken Stock (see page 14)
1–2 tablespoons chili sauce, to taste
salt and pepper
cilantro sprigs, to garnish

1 Place the pork in a bowl, add the soy sauce, vinegar, and cornstarch and stir well to mix. Pound the ginger, garlic, and chilies using a mortar and pestle or process them in a food processor.

2 Heat an empty wok until hot. Add 1 tablespoon of the oil and heat until hot. Add the red bell pepper and snow peas, sprinkle with salt and pepper to taste, and stir-fry over a moderate heat for 3 minutes. Remove with a slotted spoon and set aside.

3 Heat 2 tablespoons of the oil in the wok, add the bean curd and stir-fry over a moderate heat for 1–2 minutes until lightly colored. Remove with a slotted spoon, drain on paper towels, and keep hot.

4 Heat the remaining oil in the wok, add the pounded mixture, and stir-fry over a low heat for 2–3 minutes. Add about half of the pork, increase the heat to high and stir-fry for 2–3 minutes. Remove with a slotted spoon and set aside. Repeat with the remaining pork.

5 Pour the stock into the wok and bring to the boil, stirring, then stir in the chili sauce. Return the meat and any juices to the wok with the red bell pepper and snow peas. Stir-fry for 1–2 minutes until the meat is tender and the ingredients are hot and evenly combined. Fold in the bean curd, garnish with cilantro, and serve.

Serves 3–4
Preparation time: 15–20 minutes
Cooking time: 15–20 minutes

Mu-shu Pork

1 Wrap the pork in plastic wrap and place it in the freezer for 1–2 hours until it is just hard. Meanwhile, put the black fungus and golden needles in separate bowls and pour in about ½ cup hot water into each. Leave to soak for 30–40 minutes.

2 Drain the black fungus and cut them into thin strips, discarding any hard parts. Drain the golden needles, split them lengthways in half, and cut off any hard parts.

3 Remove the pork from the freezer and unwrap it, then cut it into thin shreds, working against the grain. Place the shreds in a nonmetallic dish, add half of the soy sauce and rice wine or sherry, the cornstarch, and sugar and stir to mix. Leave to marinate at room temperature for about 30 minutes or until the pork is completely thawed.

4 Whisk the eggs with the sesame oil and a pinch each of salt and pepper. Heat an empty wok until hot. Add 1 tablespoon of the peanut oil and heat until hot. Add the egg mixture and scramble over a moderate heat for about 5 minutes until set. Turn the scrambled eggs on to a plate and separate them into small pieces. Set aside.

5 Heat the remaining oil in the wok and stir-fry the pork in two batches over a high heat for 3–5 minutes for each batch. Return all of the pork to the wok, add the scallions, black fungus, golden needles, and the remaining soy sauce and rice wine or sherry. Toss vigorously to combine all the ingredients together, then add the scrambled egg pieces and toss again. Serve immediately, sprinkled with sesame oil.

Cook's Notes

Dried black fungus and golden needles are sold in plastic packets in Chinese supermarkets. Cloud ears and wood ears are other names for black fungus. In China, they are highly regarded for their crunchy texture and nutritional value—they are rich in minerals and protein. Golden needles are dried tiger lily buds, used in stir-fries for their color and fragrance.

Serves 3–4
Preparation time: 15–20 minutes, plus freezing and marinating
Cooking time: about 15 minutes

I pork fillet (tenderloin), weighing about 12 oz.
½ oz. dried black fungus
½ oz. dried golden needles (tiger lily buds)
2 tablespoons soy sauce
2 tablespoons rice wine or dry sherry
2 teaspoons cornstarch
½ teaspoon sugar
2 eggs
I teaspoon sesame oil, plus a little more to finish
3 tablespoons peanut oil
4 scallions, thinly sliced on the diagonal
salt and pepper

Twice-cooked Pork

4 boneless pork sparerib chops
2 bunches of scallions
2 inch piece of fresh ginger
2 tablespoons soy sauce
4 tablespoons rice wine or dry
   sherry
2 tablespoons peanut oil
2 garlic cloves, finely chopped
3 heaped tablespoons plum sauce
salt and pepper

The method of twice-cooking is often used for belly of pork because it is a fatty cut of meat. In the first cooking, the pork is simmered to render the fat, then the meat that is left is stir-fried to make it crisp. Here, less fatty sparerib chops are given the twice-cooked treatment, and the end result is exceptionally good.

1 Put the chops in a single layer in a flameproof casserole and cover with cold water. Roughly chop 4 of the scallions and peel and slice half of the ginger, then add them to the pan with the soy sauce, half of the rice wine or sherry, and a little salt and pepper. Bring to a boil, cover, and simmer very gently for 30 minutes. Lift the pork out of the cooking liquid and let it cool.
2 Meanwhile, slice the remaining scallions thinly on the diagonal and finely chop the remaining ginger.
3 Cut the pork into thin slices, working against the grain. Heat an empty wok until hot. Add the oil and heat until hot. Add about half of the pork and stir-fry over a high heat for 3–5 minutes until nicely browned and crispy. Remove with a slotted spoon and repeat with the remaining pork.
4 Add the remaining scallions and ginger to the wok with the garlic and stir to mix, then add the plum sauce, the remaining rice wine or sherry, and a few tablespoonfuls of water. Stir-fry to mix, then return all of the pork to the wok and toss vigorously over a high heat for about 1 minute until the pork and scallions are glazed with sauce. Serve immediately.

Cook's Notes
You can do the first cooking up to 24 hours in advance. Once the meat has cooled, wrap it well, then keep it in the refrigerator until you are ready to do the second cooking.

Plum sauce is often used as a dipping sauce for duck and pork, but it is very useful in stir-fries for a quick, ready-made sauce.

Serves 3–4
Preparation time: 20 minutes, plus cooling
Cooking time: about 50 minutes

Stir-fried Pork with Cucumber

1 cucumber
2 tablespoons peanut oil
1 onion, thinly sliced
1 inch piece of fresh ginger, peeled
    and cut into matchsticks
12 oz. pork fillet (tenderloin), cut
    into thin strips against the grain
salt and pepper
SAUCE:
1 tablespoon cornstarch
½ cup cold Chicken Stock (see
    page 14) or water
2 tablespoons soy sauce
2 tablespoons rice wine or
    dry sherry

1 Trim off the ends of the cucumber, then cut the cucumber crossways into 6 equal pieces. Cut each of these pieces into quarters lengthways, then cut out and discard the seeds.
2 Prepare the sauce. Blend the cornstarch in a small bowl with 2 tablespoons of the stock or water, then add the remaining sauce ingredients.
3 Heat an empty wok until hot. Add the oil and heat until hot. Add the onion and ginger and stir-fry over a low heat for a few seconds, then add the pork strips, increase the heat and stir-fry for 3–4 minutes.
4 Pour in the sauce and bring to a boil over a high heat, stirring constantly until thickened and glossy. Add the cucumber and stir-fry for 1–2 minutes or until the pork is tender and the cucumber is hot. Add salt and pepper to taste and serve immediately.

Serves 3–4
Preparation time: 15–20 minutes
Cooking time: about 15 minutes

Sichuan Pork

4 tablespoons peanut oil
1 lb. pork fillet (tenderloin), cut
    into thin strips against the grain
1 green bell pepper, cored,
    deseeded, and cut lengthways
    into thin strips
1 inch piece of fresh ginger, peeled
    and finely chopped
2 garlic cloves, finely chopped
2 green chilies, roughly chopped,
    seeds discarded according
    to taste
8 oz. can sliced bamboo shoots,
    drained
SAUCE:
2 teaspoons cornstarch
6 tablespoons Chicken Stock
    (see page 14) or water
2 tablespoons chili sauce
2 tablespoons rice wine or dry
    sherry
1 tablespoon soy sauce
2 teaspoons dark brown sugar
pinch of salt

Sichuan dishes are hot and spicy, so include as many of the fresh chili seeds in this dish as you dare.

1 Prepare the sauce. Blend the cornstarch in a measuring cup with 2 tablespoons of the stock or water, then add the remaining sauce ingredients.
2 Heat an empty wok until hot. Add half of the oil and heat until hot. Add the pork and stir-fry in batches over a high heat for 3–4 minutes, then transfer the pork to a plate using a slotted spoon.
3 Heat the remaining oil in the wok, then add the green bell pepper, ginger, garlic, and chilies. Stir-fry over a moderate heat for 1–2 minutes, then pour in the sauce mixture and bring to the boil, stirring constantly until thickened and glossy.
4 Return the meat and any juices to the wok, add the bamboo shoots, and stir-fry over a high heat for 1–2 minutes until the meat is tender and the bamboo shoots are hot. Serve immediately.

Serves 4
Preparation time: 10–15 minutes
Cooking time: 20 minutes

Sweet & Sour Pork

This is a modern version of the well-known classic dish. It has a light, crispy batter and a fresh, fruity sauce.

1 Whisk the cornstarch in a shallow dish with the soy sauce. Add the cubes of pork and stir well to mix. Cover and set aside.
2 Prepare the sauce. Blend the cornstarch in a measuring cup with the cold water, then add the pineapple juice, rice wine or sherry, sugar, soy sauce, and tomato paste. Stir well to combine. Heat the oil in a heavy-based saucepan, add the pepper strips and stir-fry for 2–3 minutes until slightly softened. Pour in the cornstarch mixture and bring to the boil over a high heat, stirring constantly until thickened and glossy. Stir in the chopped pineapple, then cover the pan and remove from the heat.
3 Heat the oil in a wok until very hot but not smoking. Add the beaten egg to the pork and stir to coat. Lift out a few cubes of pork with a slotted spoon and lower them into the hot oil. Deep-fry for 3–4 minutes until golden and crisp. Lift out with a slotted spoon and keep hot on paper towels while deep-frying the remainder.
4 Quickly reheat the sauce until bubbling. Place the cubes of pork in a warmed serving dish and pour the sauce over them. Serve immediately.

Serves 4
Preparation time: 15–20 minutes
Cooking time: about 30 minutes

1 tablespoon cornstarch
2 teaspoons soy sauce
1 lb. pork fillet (tenderloin), cut into bite-sized cubes
about 2 cups peanut oil, for deep-frying
1 egg, beaten
SAUCE:
2 teaspoons cornstarch
2 tablespoons water
8 oz. can pineapple slices in natural juice, drained and chopped, with juice reserved
2 tablespoons rice wine or dry sherry
2 tablespoons dark brown sugar
2 tablespoons soy sauce
1 tablespoon tomato paste
1 tablespoon peanut oil
1 small red bell pepper, cored, deseeded, and cut into strips
1 small green bell pepper, cored, deseeded, and cut into strips

'Have no friends not equal to yourself.'

Confucius

Spicy Pork Meatballs

½ lb. ground pork
6 oz. canned white crabmeat in brine
2 inch piece of fresh ginger, peeled and grated or finely chopped
2 garlic cloves, crushed
2 large red chilies, deseeded and finely chopped
2 handfuls of fresh cilantro leaves, roughly chopped
3 tablespoons soy sauce
2 tablespoons cornstarch
about ¾ cup peanut oil, for frying
2 cups hot Chicken Stock (see page 14)
1 teaspoon sugar
6–7 oz. Chinese cabbage leaves
salt and pepper
TO FINISH:
1 large red chili, deseeded and finely sliced
4 scallions, shredded

This recipe is based on the classic dish called Lion's Head, in which large meatballs are braised in a traditional sandpot and served on a bed of cabbage—the meatball is supposed to resemble a lion's head and the cabbage his mane.

1 Put the pork into a bowl. Drain the crab meat into a sieve and squeeze it with your hands to extract as much liquid as possible. Add the crab meat to the bowl with half of the ginger, garlic, chilies, and cilantro, and 1 tablespoon of the soy sauce. Season well with salt and pepper.

2 With your hands, mix everything together well, squeezing the mixture so that it sticks together. With wet hands, form the mixture into 24 balls. Coat the meatballs in the cornstarch.

3 Heat the oil in a wok until very hot but not smoking. Add one-third of the meatballs and fry for 2–3 minutes until they are golden and crispy on all sides. Remove with a slotted spoon and drain on paper towels. Repeat with the remaining meatballs.

4 Very carefully pour off all the oil from the wok. Wipe the wok clean with paper towels. Return all of the meatballs to the wok and sprinkle with the remaining ginger, garlic, and chili. Pour in the hot stock and the remaining soy sauce, sprinkle with the sugar and salt and pepper to taste, and bring to a gentle simmer. Cover and cook gently for 15 minutes, turning the meatballs over occasionally.

5 Tear the Chinese cabbage leaves into shreds and add them to the wok, stirring them gently into the liquid. Simmer for a further 5 minutes. Serve hot, sprinkled with the remaining cilantro, the chili strips, and scallions.

Serves 4–6
Preparation time: 30 minutes
Cooking time: 35–40 minutes

vegetables

Food lovers everywhere should pay tribute to the high status of vegetable dishes in Chinese cuisine. For where else are vegetables cooked with such sympathy and care? Bok choy, bean sprouts, spinach, carrots, onions, water chestnuts, mushrooms, and perfectly formed miniature vegetables are handled with sheer style and respect for their freshness and crisp texture. Chinese vegetables are never over-cooked; their health-giving virtues are never destroyed. All their natural goodness is preserved and enhanced.

Stir-fried Bok Choy

12 oz. bok choy
2 tablespoons peanut oil
2 garlic cloves, finely chopped
2 teaspoons sugar
2 dried red chilies
1 tablespoon soy sauce
1 tablespoon rice wine vinegar or
    white wine or cider vinegar
salt
sesame oil, to finish

This is a quick and simple stir-fry that goes well with meat and poultry dishes. The flavor of the bok choy with seasonings is quite distinctive.

1 Trim the white stalks of the bok choy, then cut the stalks into 1½ inch lengths. Tear or coarsely shred the green leaves.
2 Heat an empty wok until hot. Add the peanut oil and heat until hot. Add the bok-choy stalks, garlic, sugar, and salt to taste. Crumble the dried chilies over the bok choy and stir-fry over a moderate to high heat for 2 minutes.
3 Add the bok-choy leaves, soy sauce, and vinegar and toss vigorously for 30–60 seconds until the leaves start to wilt. Serve immediately, sprinkled with sesame oil.

Cook's Notes

Bok choy, which you may also see labeled as bok choi and pak choi, can be bought in Asian markets and most supermarkets. It is a good-looking vegetable, which has pure white crunchy stalks and contrasting dark green leaves. A member of the mustard family, its flavor is slightly and pleasantly bitter.

Serves 3–4
Preparation time: 10 minutes
Cooking time: about 5 minutes

'When you have faults, do not fear to abandon them.'

Confucius

Green Beans with Broccoli & Almonds

2 teaspoons cornstarch
6 tablespoons vegetable stock
  or water
2 tablespoons soy sauce
1 tablespoon lemon juice
4 tablespoons flaked almonds
2 tablespoons peanut oil
6 oz. broccoli, separated
  into small florets
6 oz. green beans, diagonally cut
  into 1½–2 inch lengths
3 garlic cloves, crushed
pepper

1 Blend the cornstarch in a small bowl with 2 tablespoons of the stock or water, then add the remaining stock or water and the soy sauce and lemon juice. Stir well to combine.
2 Dry-roast the flaked almonds in a wok over a moderate heat for 1–2 minutes until lightly toasted, then remove them and set aside.
3 Heat the oil in the wok until hot, add the broccoli and stir-fry for 3 minutes. Add the beans and garlic and stir-fry for 3–4 minutes.
4 Pour in the cornstarch mixture and bring to a boil over high heat, stirring constantly until thickened and glossy. Add pepper to taste and serve immediately, sprinkled with the toasted almonds.

Serves 4
Preparation time: 10–15 minutes
Cooking time: about 12 minutes

Buddha's Pot

3 tablespoons peanut oil
10 oz. firm bean curd (tofu),
  drained, dried, and cubed
12 oz. bag vegetable stir-fry mix
8 oz Chinese cabbage, shredded
2 tablespoons soy sauce
2 teaspoons lemon juice
salt and pepper

1 Heat an empty wok until hot. Add 2 tablespoons of the oil and heat until hot. Add the bean curd cubes and stir-fry for 2–3 minutes until lightly colored on all sides. Remove with a slotted spoon and drain on paper towels.
2 Heat the remaining oil in the wok until hot. Add the vegetable mix and cook according to package instructions, then add the Chinese cabbage, soy sauce, lemon juice, and salt and pepper to taste. Increase the heat to high and stir-fry for 2–3 minutes until all the ingredients are hot and evenly combined. Add the bean curd, fold in gently and serve immediately.

Cook's Notes
Bags of vegetable stir-fry mix are available at supermarkets. There is a huge variety to choose from, and they are an absolute boon to the busy cook because all the time-consuming preparation of vegetables is done for you.

Serves 4
Preparation time: 5 minutes
Cooking time: about 10 minutes

Sweet Spinach with Garlic & Sesame Seeds

1 Remove the stalks and any tough ribs from the spinach. Put several spinach leaves on top of each other, roll them up together into a cigar shape, then cut them crossways into shreds. Repeat with the remaining leaves.
2 Whisk the garlic in a small bowl with the soy sauce and honey.
3 Dry-roast the sesame seeds in a wok over a moderate heat for 1–2 minutes until lightly toasted, then remove them and set aside.
4 Heat the oil in the wok until hot, add the spinach and stir-fry for 1–2 minutes until the spinach just begins to wilt. Add the soy sauce mixture and stir-fry for 30 seconds. Serve immediately, sprinkled with the toasted sesame seeds.

Serves 2–4
Preparation time: 10 minutes
Cooking time: about 6 minutes

8 oz. spinach leaves
3–4 garlic cloves, crushed
2 tablespoons soy sauce
2 teaspoons honey
2 tablespoons sesame seeds
2 tablespoons sesame oil

Baby Vegetable Stir-fry with Orange & Oyster Sauce

2 tablespoons peanut oil
6 oz. baby carrots
6 oz. baby corn
6 oz. small button mushrooms
salt and pepper
cilantro leaves, to garnish
egg noodles, to serve
SAUCE:
2 teaspoons cornstarch
4 tablespoons cold water
finely grated rind and juice of
   I large orange
2 tablespoons oyster sauce
I tablespoon rice wine or dry
   sherry

1 Prepare the sauce. Blend the cornstarch in a small bowl with the cold water, then add the orange rind and juice, the oyster sauce, and rice wine or sherry. Stir well to combine.
2 Heat an empty wok until hot. Add the oil and heat until hot. Add the carrots and corn and stir-fry for 5 minutes, then add the mushrooms and stir-fry for 3–4 minutes.
3 Pour in the sauce mixture and bring to the boil over a high heat, stirring constantly until thickened and glossy. Add salt and pepper to taste. Garnish with cilantro leaves and serve with egg noodles.

Serves 4
Preparation time: 5 minutes
Cooking time: about 12 minutes

'The superior man is distressed by his want of ability.'

Confucius

Sesame Snow Peas

2 tablespoons sesame seeds
2 tablespoons peanut oil
2 inch piece of fresh ginger, peeled
    and finely chopped
2 garlic cloves, crushed
1 lb. snow peas, trimmed
7 oz. canned water chestnuts,
    drained and thinly sliced
2 tablespoons soy sauce
1 tablespoon sesame oil
pepper

1 Dry-roast the sesame seeds in a wok over a moderate heat for 1–2 minutes or until lightly toasted, then remove them and set aside.
2 Add the peanut oil and heat until hot. Add the ginger and garlic and stir-fry over a low heat for 1–2 minutes to flavor the oil, taking care not to let the ginger and garlic brown.
3 Add the snow peas, increase the heat to high and stir-fry for 2 minutes. Add the water chestnuts, soy sauce, and sesame oil and season with pepper. Serve immediately, sprinkled with the toasted sesame seeds.

Serves 4–6
Preparation time: 10 minutes
Cooking time: about 8 minutes

Sichuan Eggplant

2 tablespoons peanut oil
12 oz. eggplant, cut lengthwise
    into ¼ inch thick slices, then
    crossways into ¼ inch strips
½ inch piece of fresh ginger, peeled
    and cut into thin slivers
1 garlic clove, cut into thin slivers
1 fresh green chili, finely chopped,
    seeds discarded according to
    taste
2 scallions, cut into 2 inch
    matchsticks
1 tablespoon rice wine vinegar or
    white wine or cider vinegar
1 teaspoon sesame oil
SAUCE:
2 tablespoons vegetable stock
    or water
1 tablespoon soy sauce
1 teaspoon yellow bean sauce
1 teaspoon sugar

1 Blend the sauce ingredients in a small bowl.
2 Heat an empty wok until hot. Add the peanut oil and heat until hot. Add the eggplant strips and stir-fry for 1–2 minutes. Remove with a slotted spoon and set aside.
3 Add the ginger, garlic, and chili and stir-fry for 30–60 seconds to blend the flavors without browning the ingredients. Pour in the sauce mixture and bring to the boil over a high heat, stirring constantly until thickened.
4 Return the eggplant strips to the wok and stir-fry for 2 minutes. Add the scallions and toss to combine. Sprinkle with the vinegar and sesame oil and serve immediately.

Serves 4
Preparation time: 10 minutes
Cooking time: about 8 minutes

Mixed Vegetable & Tofu Stir-fry

The combination of fresh vegetables and bean curd (tofu) makes this a nutritious vegetarian main course, especially if it is served with rice.

1 Blend the cornstarch in a small bowl with 2 tablespoons of the stock or water, then add the remaining stock or water, the soy sauce, and star anise. Stir well to combine.

2 Heat an empty wok until hot. Add half of the oil and heat until hot. Add the onion and beans and stir-fry for 2 minutes. Add the celery and stir-fry for 2 minutes, then add the bell peppers and daikon and stir-fry for 2 minutes. Remove from the wok and set aside.

3 Heat the remaining oil in the wok, add the ginger and garlic and stir-fry over a low heat for 2–3 minutes to blend the flavors without browning the ingredients. Pour in the cornstarch mixture and bring to the boil over a high heat, stirring constantly until thickened and glossy. Discard the star anise.

4 Return the vegetables to the wok, toss over a high heat, then add the bean curd and stir-fry for 2–3 minutes until heated through and evenly combined with the vegetables. Serve immediately.

Serves 4
Preparation time: 15 minutes
Cooking time: about 15 minutes

2 teaspoons cornstarch
8 tablespoons vegetable stock
    or water
3 tablespoons soy sauce
2 star anise
2 tablespoons peanut oil
1 small onion, thinly sliced
4 oz. green beans, cut into
    1½ inch lengths
2 celery sticks, thinly sliced on
    the diagonal
½ each red, yellow, and green bell
    peppers, cut into 1½ inch strips
4 oz. daikon (Japanese radish),
    peeled, cut into thin 1½ inch
    strips
1 inch piece of fresh ginger, peeled
    and crushed
1 garlic clove, crushed
10 oz. firm bean curd (tofu),
    drained, dried, and cut into
    1½ inch strips

Stir-fried Mushrooms

2 tablespoons peanut oil
1 onion, finely chopped
2 carrots, very finely sliced on the diagonal
4 oz. fresh shiitake mushrooms, sliced lengthways
4 oz. fresh button mushrooms, sliced lengthways
4 garlic cloves, finely chopped
4 tablespoons oyster sauce
2 tablespoons rice wine or dry sherry (optional)
4 tablespoons cold water
1 bunch of chives, coarsely chopped
salt and pepper
egg thread noodles, to serve

Shiitake and button mushrooms are chosen here for the difference in their shapes, textures, and flavors, but you can mix and match other types of mushroom according to preference and availability. If you prefer, you can use three or four different types.

1 Heat an empty wok until hot. Add the oil and heat until hot, then. Add the onion and carrots and stir-fry for 1–2 minutes. Add the shiitake and button mushrooms, garlic, and plenty of salt and pepper and toss vigorously over a medium to high heat for 2–3 minutes.

2 Add the oyster sauce and rice wine or dry sherry, if using, then the cold water. Stir-fry for another 3 minutes, then add half of the chives. Toss for 1 minute only. Serve hot on a bed of egg thread noodles, sprinkled with the remaining chives.

Cook's Notes
Fresh shiitake mushrooms are sold in many supermarkets. They have a rich earthy flavor and firm texture.

Serves 4–6
Preparation time: 10–15 minutes
Cooking time: about 10 minutes

'The people may be able to follow a course of action, but they may not be made to understand it.'

Confucius

Crunchy Sweet & Sour Vegetables

2 tablespoons peanut oil
2 carrots, thinly sliced on the
    diagonal
1 head of fennel, thinly sliced, with
    leaves reserved for garnish
1 red bell pepper, cored, deseeded,
    and cut into ½ inch squares
1 green bell pepper, cored,
    deseeded, and cut into ½ inch
    squares
¾ cup unsalted cashew nuts
3 oz. ready-made sweet and sour
    sauce
7 oz. canned pineapple slices in
    natural juice, drained and cut
    into chunks

1 Heat an empty wok until hot. Add the oil and heat until hot. Add the carrots, fennel, peppers, and nuts. Stir-fry for 2 minutes, then add the sweet and sour sauce. Bring to a boil, stirring, then add the pineapple chunks and stir-fry for 2 minutes more, until the pineapple is hot.
2 Serve immediately, sprinkled with the reserved fennel leaves.

Serves 4
Preparation time: 10 minutes
Cooking time: 7–8 minutes

Vegetable Chow Mein

8 oz. dried thread or fine egg
    noodles
2 tablespoons peanut oil
2 carrots, cut into matchsticks
1 green bell pepper, cored,
    deseeded, and cut lengthways
    into thin strips
3 celery sticks, cut into
    matchsticks
7 oz. canned water chestnuts,
    drained and cut into
    matchsticks
6 oz. Chinese cabbage leaves,
    trimmed and shredded
6 oz. spinach, trimmed and
    shredded
salt and pepper
SAUCE:
2 teaspoons cornstarch
4 tablespoons cold water
2 tablespoons soy sauce
1 tablespoon rice wine or dry
    sherry

1 First prepare the sauce ingredients. Blend the cornstarch to a thin paste with the cold water, soy sauce, and rice wine or sherry.
2 Break the noodles into pieces with your hands, then cook them according to package instructions.
3 Meanwhile, heat an empty wok until hot. Add the oil and heat until hot. Add the carrots, green bell pepper, and celery and stir-fry for 2–3 minutes.
4 Stir the sauce to mix, then pour it into the wok and bring to a boil, stirring constantly. Remove the wok from the heat.
5 Drain the noodles and add them to the wok. Return the wok to a high heat, add the water chestnuts, Chinese cabbage, and spinach and toss for 1–2 minutes or until all the ingredients are combined and the spinach is just wilted. Add salt and pepper to taste and serve immediately.

Serves 4
Preparation time: 10–15 minutes
Cooking time: about 8 minutes

Ma-po Tofu

This Sichuan dish was named after the lady who invented it, a restaurateur's wife whose face was pock-marked—Ma-Po means pock-marked woman. Despite its unfortunate associations, it makes an excellent vegetarian main course. For the most delicious and nutritious meal, serve it with plain boiled rice.

1 Soak the dried mushrooms in the hot water for 35–40 minutes. Drain the mushrooms into a sieve over a bowl and reserve the soaking water. Cut the mushroom caps into small square shapes, discarding any hard stalks.

2 Heat an empty wok until hot. Add the oil and heat until hot. Add the scallions, red and green bell peppers, garlic, chili, and mushrooms, stir-fry for 1–2 minutes, then add the black beans and black bean sauce, the rice wine or sherry, the mushroom soaking liquid, and the cold water. Bring to a boil and simmer for 5 minutes, then add the bean curd and stir gently to mix. Simmer for another 5 minutes, stirring occasionally. Taste for seasoning and serve hot, drizzled with chili oil.

Cook's Notes

The salted black beans are traditional, but they are not always easy to obtain unless you go to a Chinese supermarket. Black bean sauce is available in small bottles in most supermarkets, so if you can't get the black beans, simply increase the black bean sauce, according to taste.

Serves 4–6
Preparation time: 15 minutes, plus soaking
Cooking time: about 15 minutes

6 dried shiitake mushrooms
½ cup hot water
2 tablespoons peanut oil
4 scallions, cut crossways into quarters
1 small red bell pepper, cored, deseeded, and finely diced
1 small green bell pepper, cored, deseeded, and finely diced
2 garlic cloves, finely chopped
1 bird's eye chili, deseeded and very finely chopped
2 heaped tablespoons canned salted black beans, rinsed and coarsely mashed
2 tablespoons black bean sauce
2 tablespoons rice wine or dry sherry
4 tablespoons cold water
10 oz. firm bean curd (tofu), drained, dried, and cut into 1–1½ inch squares
salt and pepper
chili oil, to finish

rice

Rice and noodle dishes are staples of Chinese cooking. They feature in thousands of recipes. Rice is so important in China that it has entered the language in special ways and come to represent fundamental meanings in everyday life. For example, when someone asks you over to dinner they say, literally, "Come and have rice with me." If a friend tells you that he has "grains to chew," it means that he has a job. But if he loses his job, he has "broken the rice bowl."

Hot Tossed Rice with Shrimp & Chinese Sausage

8 oz. white long-grain rice
1–2 Chinese pork sausages, total
   weight about 4 oz.
2 eggs
1 bunch of scallions, sliced into
   thin rings
1–2 red or green chilies, finely
   chopped
4 tablespoons peanut oil
4–6 oz. cooked peeled shrimp,
   defrosted and dried thoroughly
   if frozen
4 tablespoons soy sauce, plus extra
   to serve
2 tablespoons rice wine vinegar or
   white wine or cider vinegar
1 teaspoon sugar
salt and pepper

This rice dish is substantial enough to be served as a main course. The pairing of shellfish and meat is popular all over the Orient.

1 Rinse the rice in a sieve under cold running water, then place it in a saucepan and add a good pinch of salt. Pour in enough cold water to come about 1 inch above the surface of the rice and bring to a boil.

2 Stir the rice, then place the sausage on top, cutting it to fit in the pan if necessary. Cover tightly with the lid and cook over a low heat for 15 minutes or until the rice is tender and the water absorbed. Remove the sausage from the rice and set aside. Tip the rice into a bowl and leave until cold.

3 Beat the eggs in a bowl with half of the scallions and chili and salt and pepper to taste. Heat an empty wok until hot. Add 1 teaspoon of the oil and heat until hot. Add half of the eggs and tilt the wok to make a thin flat omelette. Slide it out of the pan and roll it up into a sausage shape. Repeat with another teaspoon of oil and the remaining egg mixture.

4 Cut the sausage into tiny bite-sized pieces. Heat the remaining oil in the wok and add the sausage with the remaining scallions and chili. Stir-fry over a moderate to high heat for about 5 minutes until the sausage is browned and crispy.

5 Add the cold rice a spoonful at a time and stir-fry until the grains are separate. When all the rice is in the pan, add the shrimp and toss everything together for 1–2 minutes. Taste for seasoning.

6 Turn the rice into a warmed serving bowl. Cut the omelettes crossways into thin strips and place them on top of the rice. Mix together the soy sauce, vinegar, and sugar and drizzle it over the top. Serve immediately, with extra soy sauce for those who like it.

Cook's Notes
You can buy Chinese sausages in Asian supermarkets. They are wind-dried, thin and spicy, made with pork and liver, and sometimes with duck. If you can't get them, you can use any other kind of spicy sausage instead.

Serves 4–6
Preparation time: 15 minutes, plus cooling
Cooking time: about 30 minutes

Rainbow Rice

6 oz. white long-grain rice
2 cups cold water
2 tablespoons peanut oil
2 carrots, diced
½ bunch of scallions, finely
    chopped
1 red bell pepper, cored, deseeded,
    and diced
2 celery sticks, diced
4 oz. frozen peas
4–6 oz. slice of cooked ham, cut
    into thin strips
7 oz. can straw mushrooms in
    brine, drained and halved
    lengthwise
2 tablespoons soy sauce
1 tablespoon sesame oil
salt and pepper

1 Rinse the rice in a sieve under cold running water, then put it in a medium saucepan. Add the cold water and ½ teaspoon salt and bring to the boil. Stir once, cover with a lid and simmer for 15 minutes or until the rice is tender and has absorbed the water. Turn the rice into a sieve and rinse under cold running water until cold.
2 Heat an empty wok until hot. Add the peanut oil and heat until hot. Add the carrots and stir-fry for 2 minutes, then add the spring onions, red pepper, and celery and stir-fry for 2 minutes. Add the frozen peas and ham, increase the heat to high and stir-fry for 2–3 minutes, then add the mushrooms and toss until piping hot.
3 Add the rice and stir-fry until it is evenly mixed with the ham and vegetables, using chopsticks to help separate the grains of rice. Add pepper to taste, sprinkle with the soy sauce and sesame oil and serve immediately.

Serves 3–4
Preparation time: 10 minutes
Cooking time: about 25 minutes

Egg Fried Rice

8 oz. white long-grain rice
2½ cups cold water
2 eggs
4 scallions, finely chopped
2½ tablespoons peanut oil
4 oz. frozen peas
4 tablespoons soy sauce
4 oz. bean sprouts
4 oz. slice of cooked ham,
    shredded
salt and pepper

1 Cook the rice as in step 1 of Rainbow Rice, above.
2 Beat the eggs with half of the scallions and season to taste. Heat an empty wok until hot. Add 2 teaspoons of the oil and heat until hot. Add the egg and scallion mixture and stir over a low heat until the eggs are scrambled. Put the scrambled eggs in a bowl.
3 Heat the remaining oil in the wok until hot. Add the remaining scallions, the peas, and half of the soy sauce, increase the heat to moderate and stir-fry for 2–3 minutes or until the peas are cooked.
4 Add the bean sprouts and stir-fry for 1 minute, then add the cold rice, ham, and the remaining soy sauce. Toss for 1 minute to separate the grains of rice, then add the scrambled eggs and toss again until all the ingredients are combined and piping hot. Taste and adjust the seasoning if necessary. Serve immediately.

Serves 3–4
Preparation time: 10 minutes
Cooking time: about 25 minutes

Ants Climbing Trees

This strange-sounding dish gets its name from the ground pork (ants) clinging to the trees (noodles). In this recipe, transparent or cellophane noodles are used. Made from mung beans, they are sold in skeins like wool. They can be bought in oriental stores, but if you have difficulty in getting them, you can use egg noodles instead.

1 Soak the noodles in hot water for 30 minutes or according to package instructions.

2 Meanwhile, make the marinade. Put all the ingredients into a shallow dish, add the ground pork, and stir well to mix. Leave to marinate for about 30 minutes.

3 Drain the noodles. Heat an empty wok until hot. Add the oil and heat until hot. Add the scallions and stir-fry for 30 seconds or until softened, taking care not to let them brown. Add the pork with the marinade, increase the heat to high and stir-fry for 3–4 minutes or until the pork loses its pink color.

4 Pour in the stock and bring it to the boil, stirring constantly. Add the drained noodles and toss until all of the liquid is absorbed and the noodles are piping hot. Serve immediately.

Cook's Notes
This dish is quite spicy, but if you like your food really hot, add more chili sauce, or add 1–2 finely chopped fresh chilies to the pork mixture when stir-frying in step 3.

Serves 3–4
Preparation time: 10 minutes, plus soaking and marinating
Cooking time: 10 minutes

8 oz. transparent or cellophane noodles
8 oz. ground pork
2 tablespoons peanut oil
4 scallions, thinly sliced on the diagonal
¾ cup hot Chicken Stock (see page 14)
MARINADE:
2 tablespoons soy sauce
1 tablespoon rice wine or dry sherry
1 tablespoon peanut oil
2 teaspoons hot chili sauce
1 teaspoon sesame oil
½ teaspoon sugar

'Above ground I will be food for kites, below I shall be food for mole-crickets and ants. Why rob one to feed the other?'

Juang-zu

Noodles with Chicken and Shrimp

1 oz. dried shiitake mushrooms
¾ cup hot water
1 lb. dried egg noodles
2 tablespoons peanut oil
6 oz. boneless, skinless chicken
    breast, diced
1 garlic clove, crushed
2 slices of fresh ginger, peeled and
    chopped
4 scallions, diagonally sliced into
    ½ inch pieces
6 oz. raw shrimp, peeled
2 tablespoons soy sauce
2 tablespoons rice wine or dry
    sherry
3 cups Chicken Stock (see p. 14)
2 tablespoons cornstarch
2 oz. cooked ham, shredded
salt

1 Soak the dried mushrooms in the hot water for 35–40 minutes. Meanwhile, cook the egg noodles according to package instructions until they are just tender. Drain and divide between 6 deep bowls. Keep warm.

2 Drain the mushrooms into a sieve. Slice the mushroom caps thinly.

3 Heat an empty wok until hot. Add the oil and heat until hot. Add the chicken, garlic, and ginger and stir-fry over a moderate to high heat for 2–3 minutes. Add the scallions and mushrooms and stir-fry for 2 minutes.

4 Add the shrimp, soy sauce, rice wine or sherry, ½ teaspoon salt, and the stock. Bring to the boil over a high heat, then simmer for 5 minutes. Blend the cornstarch to a paste with a little cold water, then pour into the liquid in the wok and stir until it thickens slightly.

5 Pour the chicken and shrimp over the noodles, sprinkle with the shredded ham, and serve immediately.

Serves 6
Preparation time: 20 minutes, plus soaking
Cooking time: 20 minutes

*'The superior man is satisfied and composed;
the mean man is always full of distress.'*

Confucius

Hot-tossed Noodles with Spicy Meat Sauce

2 tablespoons peanut oil
I small onion, finely chopped
I fresh chili, deseeded and very
    finely chopped
2 garlic cloves, very finely chopped
8 oz. ground beef
I cup beef stock
2 tablespoons soy sauce, or more
    to taste
2 tablespoons tomato paste
I tablespoon rice wine or dry
    sherry
½ teaspoon sugar
8 oz. medium egg noodles
salt and pepper

1 Heat an empty wok until hot. Add the oil and heat until hot.
Add the onion, chili, and garlic and stir-fry over a low heat for
2–3 minutes until softened. Add the meat, increase the heat to
moderate, and stir-fry for 5 minutes or until it loses its pink color.
2 Add all of the remaining ingredients except the noodles and
season to taste with salt and pepper. Bring to the boil, stirring, then
lower the heat and simmer for 10–15 minutes until thickened,
stirring frequently.
3 Meanwhile, cook the noodles according to package instructions.
Drain, then turn them into a warmed large bowl.
4 Taste the sauce for seasoning and add more soy sauce if liked. Add
the meat sauce to the bowl of noodles and toss quickly to mix. Serve
immediately.

Serves 4
Preparation time: 10 minutes
Cooking time: about 25 minutes

Velvet Noodles

½ oz. dried shiitake mushrooms
¾ in. hot water
8 oz. medium egg noodles
2 tablespoons peanut oil
4 oz. broccoli, separated
    into small florets
4 oz. carrots, cut into matchsticks
2 garlic cloves, crushed
½ red bell pepper, cored,
    deseeded, and finely diced
½ green bell pepper, cored,
    deseeded, and finely diced
I tablespoon sesame oil, to finish
SAUCE:
6 tablespoons vegetable stock
    or water
2 tablespoons soy sauce
I teaspoon five-spice powder
½ teaspoon ground ginger

1 Soak the dried mushrooms in the hot water for 35–40 minutes.
Meanwhile, cook and drain the noodles according to package
instructions. Blend the sauce ingredients in a small bowl.
2 Drain the mushrooms in a sieve, then chop them finely.
3 Heat an empty wok until hot. Add the peanut oil and heat until
hot. Add the mushrooms, broccoli, and carrots and stir-fry for 3–4
minutes, then add the garlic and peppers and pour in the sauce
mixture. Bring to the boil over a high heat, stirring constantly.
4 Add the drained noodles and toss them over a high heat until they
are hot and evenly combined with the vegetables. Serve immediately,
sprinkled with the sesame oil.

Serves 4
Preparation time: 15 minutes, plus soaking
Cooking time: about 10 minutes

Chicken Chow Mein

Chow mein was originally invented by Chinese immigrants in the United States. Literally translated it means "stir-fried noodles," but there are no hard-and-fast rules for making it, and you can add anything to the noodles you like—meat, fish, or vegetables.

1 Cook the rice noodles according to package instructions.

2 Meanwhile, prepare the sauce. Blend the cornstarch to a paste with 2 tablespoons of the stock or water, then stir in the remaining stock or water, the soy sauce, rice wine or sherry, and the sesame oil.

3 Drain the noodles, rinse under cold water, and set aside.

4 Heat an empty wok until hot. Add the oil and heat until hot. Add the scallions, ginger, and garlic and stir-fry for 1–2 minutes or until softened, taking care not to let the ingredients brown. Add the chicken, increase the heat to high and stir-fry for 3–4 minutes or until lightly colored on all sides.

5 Add the snow peas and stir-fry for 1–2 minutes or until just tender, then add the ham and bean sprouts and stir-fry to mix. Stir the sauce, pour it into the wok and bring to a boil, stirring constantly. Add the drained noodles and toss until combined and piping hot. Add pepper to taste and serve immediately.

Serves 4
Preparation time: 15 minutes
Cooking time: 20 minutes

8 oz. Chinese rice noodles (*mihun*)
2 tablespoons peanut oil
3–4 scallions, thinly sliced
    on the diagonal
1 inch piece of fresh ginger, peeled
    and finely chopped
1 garlic clove, crushed
2 boneless, skinless chicken
    breasts, each weighing about
    5 oz, cut into thin strips against
    the grain
4 oz. snow peas, trimmed
4 oz. slice of cooked ham,
    shredded
3 oz. bean sprouts
pepper
SAUCE:
2 teaspoons cornstarch
8 tablespoons Chicken Stock
    (see page 14) or water
2 tablespoons soy sauce
2 tablespoons rice wine or dry
    sherry
2 teaspoons sesame oil

desserts

Chinese desserts are generally simple and fresh—they will freshen your mouth and lighten the mood at the end of a meal. They are usually based on fresh fruits such as apples, bananas, lychees, mandarin oranges, peaches, pineapples, pears, mangoes, and plums, sometimes lightly poached. Fruit is also frequently served as deep-fried fritters in a luscious batter. Occasionally, a delicate almond-flavored jelly will appear, as smooth as silk.

Fragrant Fruit Salad

3 oz. sugar
2 pieces of star anise
1 cinnamon stick
1 scant cup cold water
1 ripe pineapple
2 ripe mangoes
8 oz. (½ lb.) lychees
4 tablespoons rice wine or dry
   sherry
TO DECORATE:
star anise
cape gooseberries (physalis)
pineapple leaves

Serve this fresh fruit salad well chilled at the end of a Chinese meal. You will find its sweetness and coolness most refreshing, especially if the previous courses were hot and spicy.

1 Put the sugar, star anise, and cinnamon stick into a heavy saucepan and pour in the cold water. Heat gently until the sugar has dissolved, then boil without stirring for 2 minutes. Remove from the heat, cover and leave to cool.

2 Meanwhile, prepare the fruit. Remove the skin and eyes from the pineapple, then cut the fruit lengthways into quarters. Cut away the hard woody core, then slice the flesh crossways into bite-sized pieces. Cut the mangoes lengthways into 3 pieces, avoiding the long central stone. Cut a crosshatch design inside the two rounded pieces of mango, then push them inside out so that the squares of flesh stand out. Slice off the squares of flesh. Cut the remaining mango flesh from around the stone, then cut it into bite-sized pieces. Peel the rough skin off the lychees with a knife, make a long slit down one side of each fruit and remove the stone.

3 Put the fruit into a large bowl, strain the sugar syrup over it and add the rice wine or sherry. Stir gently to mix. Cover tightly and chill in the refrigerator for at least 4 hours. Before serving, decorate the fruit salad with whole star anise, cape gooseberries, and pineapple leaves. To expose the orange fruit of the cape gooseberries, open the papery husks and pull them back from the fruit, turning the husks inside out. Twist the husks very tightly at the base so that they stay put.

Cook's Notes
To save time, buy tubs of ready-prepared fresh pineapple and mango packed in their own natural juice. They are sold in the refrigerated sections of the produce departments in most large supermarkets. Fresh lychees are seasonal, and are usually to be found in Asian markets in the winter months leading up to Christmas. If you can't get them, used canned lychees, which are also very good.

   Cape gooseberries, while widely available in Asia and Europe, are not readily available in the United States. Try carambolas, also known as star fruit, which offer a similar sweet/tart taste and an exotic appearance.

Serves 6
Preparation time: 30 minutes, plus chilling
Cooking time: 3–4 minutes

Almond Jelly

1 tablespoon powdered gelatin
4 tablespoons cold water
¾ cup evaporated milk
about 1½ cup whole or 2% milk
3 tablespoons superfine sugar
2 teaspoons almond extract

1 Sprinkle the gelatin powder over the cold water in a small heatproof bowl. Leave to stand for 5 minutes until spongy, then stand the bowl in a saucepan of gently simmering water and stir for a few minutes over a low heat until the gelatin has dissolved. Remove the bowl from the pan.

2 Pour the evaporated milk into a 2-cup measuring cup and fill up to the 2-cup mark with ordinary milk. Heat the two kinds of milk with the sugar until hot, then slowly pour in the dissolved gelatin, stirring constantly. Add the almond extract and stir again.

3 Pour the mixture into 4–6 small dishes or ramekins. Leave to cool, then cover and chill in the refrigerator for at least 6 hours until set.

Cook's Notes

Only use pure, natural almond extract. Synthetic almond extract does not taste good in uncooked desserts like this one.

Serves 4–6
Preparation time: 20 minutes, plus cooling and chilling
Cooking time: about 5 minutes

Fruit Fritters

½ cup all-purpose flour
½ cup cornstarch
1 heaped tablespoon superfine
    sugar, plus extra for sprinkling
1 large egg, separated
a scant ½ cup cold water
about 1 cup peanut oil, for deep-
    frying
about 1 lb. prepared mixed fruit
    (e.g., banana, pear, pineapple)

1 Sift the flour and cornstarch into a bowl, then add the sugar and egg yolk and stir to mix. Slowly pour in the cold water, stirring all the time, then beat with a balloon whisk until smooth. Whisk the egg white until stiff, then fold into the batter with a large nonmetal spoon until evenly incorporated.

2 Heat the oil in a wok until very hot but not smoking. Dip one piece of fruit at a time into the batter, then lower it into the hot oil. Deep-fry in batches for about 30 seconds on each side until crisp and golden, turning once. Transfer to paper towels with a slotted spoon and dredge liberally with superfine sugar. Leave the fritters for 5 minutes before serving because the fruit inside is very hot.

Serves 6–8
Preparation time: 10 minutes
Cooking time: about 15 minutes

Red Bean Paste Pancakes

This traditional dessert of stuffed, deep-fried pancakes is from northern China. It sounds rather unusual, but it is absolutely delicious.

12 small Chinese pancakes (see Cook's Notes, below)
12 tablespoons sweetened red bean paste
about 1 cup peanut oil, for deep-frying
superfine sugar, for sprinkling

1 Place one pancake on a board or work surface and spread 1 tablespoon of the red bean paste in the center. Brush water all around the edge of the pancake, then fold the rounded side nearest to you over the paste. Fold the two opposite sides into the center, then fold the top flap down. Repeat with the remaining pancakes.
2 Heat the oil in a wok until very hot but not smoking. Deep-fry the pancakes one at a time for 1–2 minutes or until crisp and golden on both sides, turning them once. Drain the pancakes on kitchen paper, then cut crossways into 6–8 strips. Serve warm, sprinkled liberally with superfine sugar.

Cook's Notes

The pancakes used for this dessert are the same as the ones served with Peking duck. Chinese cooks make their own, but ready-made "Peking duck" pancakes are sold in many large supermarkets, so there is no need for you to go to so much trouble.

Sweetened red bean paste is sold in cans in oriental supermarkets. It is a very thick paste that is a dark reddish brown in color. Once the can has been opened, place any leftover paste in an airtight container and keep it in the refrigerator or freezer. If you can't get red bean paste, you can use sweetened chestnut purée or almond paste instead.

Serves 8
Preparation time: 10 minutes
Cooking time: about 20 minutes

glossary

Bamboo shoots: sold canned in brine, these are the young shoots from the base of the bamboo plant. They are pale ivory in color, with a crisp texture and subtly sweet but bland flavor. Use them sliced in stir-fries; they only need to be heated through.

Bean curd: also known as tofu, this is a highly nutritious ingredient that is made from yellow soy-beans. It is rich in protein, low in fat, and very popular in Chinese cooking. Firm bean curd is sold in blocks, which can be sliced or diced; it is good for stir-frying and braising. Silken tofu is softer, and so best in sauces and soups. Bean curd is white and rather bland, so it is often used with colorful and flavorsome ingredients.

Bean sprouts: young, tender sprouts of mung beans used in many salads and stir-fries for their crisp texture. They can be eaten raw or cooked very briefly. Use as soon as possible after purchase as they quickly discolor and go limp.

Black beans: soybeans that have been preserved by salting and fermenting. Sold in cans, they have a very strong salty flavor and should be rinsed before use. They are used in small quantities, either whole or crushed, and go very well with the flavor of fresh ginger. Black bean sauce is a ready-made sauce that is widely available, and there are many varieties to choose from.

Black fungus: a dried fungus that also goes by the various names of cloud ears, tree ears, and wood ears. It is used more for its crunchy texture than its flavor and is rich in minerals, protein, and carbohydrates. Soak in hot water for 35–40 minutes before use.

Bok choy: also called bok choi and pak choi, this is a dark green leafy vegetable with crunchy white stalks. Its Latin name is *Brassica rapa chinensis*, and it is not the same thing as Chinese cabbage. It has a slightly bitter flavor and is excellent in stir-fries.

Chilies: fresh red and green chilies are used in Chinese cooking, especially in the western provinces. The smaller they are, the hotter they will be, and it is a matter of taste which ones you use. Dried red chilies are also used and so too is bottled chili sauce, although the latter is often used as a table condiment. Chili oil is another hot ingredient. Sprinkle it sparingly over food at the end of cooking.

Chinese cabbage: this goes by many other names, such as Chinese leaves, Pe-tsai, and Peking cabbage. The Latin name is *Brassica rapa pekinensis*, not to be confused with bok choy (pak choi). It is pale with crinkly leaves and a bland flavor, most often used in stir-fries.

Chinese chives: very long, thick chives that have a strong oniony flavour and coarse texture. They are only sold in Asian produce markets, but green scallion tops or ordinary chives can be substituted.

Chinese sausages: wind-dried, thin sausages made with pork and liver, and sometimes duck. They taste spicy and sweet, and must be cooked before eating. They are often steamed on top of rice.

Chop suey: this is believed to have been invented by Chinese immigrants in the Wild American West. The name comes from the Chinese word *zasui*, meaning "mixed bits." It is a medley of different ingredients cooked together. Ingredients vary widely, but chicken and vegetables are usually included.

Chow mein: invented by Chinese Americans, *chow mein* means "stir-fried noodles." It usually consists of some kind of meat or fish, or both, tossed with sliced vegetables and either soft or crisp egg noodles.

Cilantro: herbs are not widely used in Chinese cooking, but cilantro is an exception. It is used both chopped and as whole leaves. There really is no substitute for its pungent aroma and distinctive flavor. It is sometimes called Chinese parsley or leaf coriander.

Citrus fruit peel: this is the dried peel of oranges or tangerines. It is hard and dark in the packet, but once soaked in hot water for 30 minutes, it softens and regains some color. It is used to add an intense citrus flavor to braised dishes and stir-fries.

Daikon: an oriental radish that is long and thin. It has brown skin and white flesh and is milder and sweeter in flavor than the red radish. Cut into julienne, its crisp juicy flesh is very good in stir-fries. It is sometimes called mooli or Japanese radish.

Five-spice powder: a mixture of five ground spices: Sichuan pepper, star anise, cinnamon, cloves, and fennel. It is highly aromatic, spicy, and sweet. It is used sparingly in braised dishes and stir-fries and goes particularly well with pork and duck.

Ginger: fresh ginger root is used in many Chinese recipes, often combined with scallions, garlic, and chili. It must always be peeled and its flesh is quite fibrous, so it is a little difficult to slice and chop. One of the best ways to manage it is to keep it in the freezer. When frozen, it is easy to grate. Stem ginger is crystalized ginger packed in syrup; it is available in Asian and gourmet markets.

Golden needles: these are also called tiger lily buds, which is what they are—the dried buds of tiger lily flowers. They are used in stir-fries for their texture (they have very little flavor) and must be soaked in hot water for 30–40 minutes before use.

Hoisin sauce: a bottled sauce that is a dark reddish brown in color, thick, and smooth. Sweet and spicy, it is made from soybeans, chilies, vinegar, garlic, sugar, and other flavorings. Use it both as a table condiment and in stir-fries.

Ma-po: dishes with the name "Ma-po" are named

after a Sichuan restaurateur's wife who had a pock-marked face (*Ma-po* means "pock-marked woman"). She created a dish using bean curd, which was named after her, Ma-po Tofu. This was over a hundred years ago, but her name is still used to describe dishes that are hot and spicy.

Mein: this is the Chinese word for the snowy white transparent or cellophane noodles made from mung beans. *Mee* is the word for egg noodles, made from egg, wheat flour, and water. Available both fresh and dried, these are the noodles that are most often used in Chinese cooking.

Mu-shu: this is the Chinese name for golden needles, used to describe dishes which are garnished with them, or with yellow ingredients like scrambled egg or omelette strips, which resemble golden needles. Mu-shu Pork is one of the most famous dishes from northern China.

Oyster sauce: a bottled sauce with a unique savoriness that is used both as a table condiment and in cooking, especially in stir-fries. Although the sauce is made from oysters, it tastes surprisingly un-fishy. Brands from Hong Kong are said to be best.

Plum sauce: a sweet and glossy bottled sauce made from a special Chinese variety of plum, which is very small and sour. Plum sauce is traditionally served as a condiment with Peking duck and pancakes, but it can also be used in stir-fries; it is very good with pork and lamb.

Red bean paste: canned sweetened paste made from puréed red beans that is dark reddish brown in color and very thick. It is often used as a filling for pancakes. Once the can is open, put the paste into a bowl and keep refrigerated.

Red-cooked: refers to poultry or meat that has been slow-cooked for a long time in soy sauce so that it takes on a reddish-brown tinge.

Rice wine: made from fermented rice, this mellow wine is popular with the Chinese, both as a drink and in cooking. A dry or medium-dry sherry can be substituted.

Rice wine vinegar: this comes in red or white and is used in dipping sauces and in cooking. Red rice wine vinegar has a slightly sweeter flavor than white. Red or white wine vinegar or cider vinegar may be substituted.

Sesame oil: made from roasted white sesame seeds, this is a dark oil with a strong aroma and flavor. It is always used sparingly, most often sprinkled on food just before serving. Never stir-fry with sesame oil alone: it burns easily.

Sesame paste: this is the same thing as the Middle Eastern tahini. It is a thick, beige-brown paste made from pulped sesame seeds and is mostly used in cold dressings and dips from north and west China.

Sesame seeds: white sesame seeds are more commonly used than black. They are often toasted and sprinkled over food at the last moment

to give a crunchy bite and nutty flavor.

Shiitake mushrooms: fresh shiitake have a musky aroma, meaty flavor, and hold their shape well when cooked. These qualities make them popular in stir-fries. Dried shiitake have an intense flavor, so need only be used in small quantities. Soak in hot water before use.

Sichuan peppercorns: these are called "flower pepper" in Chinese because they are shaped like flower petals. They are not hot like real pepper, but spicy sweet. They are especially aromatic when dry-roasted before use.

Soy sauce: there are two main kinds—light and dark. Light soy has a pale color, thin consistency, and salty flavor. Dark soy sauce is darker and thicker, with a sweeter flavor. The Chinese tend to use light soy sauce more in cooking, and dark soy sauce for dips and sauces.

Spring roll wrappers: pure white, paper-thin squares of dough made from flour and water, used to wrap around savory filling mixtures to make spring rolls. They are usually 5–6 inches square and can be bought fresh or frozen. Filo pastry can be substituted, but it will need to be cut to size.

Star anise: this pretty eight-pointed spice tastes of licorice and is a main ingredient of five-spice powder. It is used whole for its strong aromatic qualities in braises and steamed dishes.

Straw mushrooms: sold canned in brine, these

mushrooms are small and delicate with pointed caps. They look pretty when halved lengthways, and are prized for their velvety texture. They take their name from the rice straw they are grown on, which is one of the reasons they are seldom seen fresh in the West. Always drain and rinse before use.

Twice-cooked: a method used with fatty cuts of meat in which the meat is first boiled to render the fat, then fried until crisp.

Velveting: a term used to describe the technique of coating meat or fish in a mixture of egg white and cornstarch before par-frying it in oil. Coating it protects the flesh, making it velvety in texture.

Water chestnuts: these are not chestnuts but tubers grown in paddy fields, readily available in cans. They have a bland flavor, but are popular for their crisp, crunchy bite.

White-cut: meat described as "white-cut" has been boiled in plain water to retain its color. It can be cooked until it is tender, or partially cooked and then left to stand in the water until cold.

Wonton wrappers: usually 3 inches round or square, these are used for making stuffed dumplings, popular for dim sum. They are made from wheat flour, egg, and water, and are yellowish in color.

Yellow bean sauce: a ready-made stir-fry sauce made from salted soybeans, soy sauce, vinegar, garlic, sugar, and seasoning.

index